Letters to the Ephesians and Timothy

GUIDANCE FOR THE CHURCH AND ITS LEADERS

BOB DEFOOR
TOM HOWE
PHIL LINEBERGER
LEIGH ANN POWERS

BAPTISTWAYPRESS®

Dallas, Texas

BAPTISTWAY PRESS® Leadership Team
Executive Director, Baptist General Convention of Texas: David Hardage
Director, Church Ministry Resources: Chris Liebrum
Director, Bible Study/Discipleship Team: Phil Miller
Publisher, BaptistWay Press®: Scott Stevens

Publishing consultant and editor: Ross West
Cover and Interior Design and Production: Desktop Miracles, Inc.
Printing: Data Reproductions Corporation

First edition: September 2014
ISBN-13: 978-1-938355-22-6

How to Make the Best Use of This Issue

Whether you're the teacher or a student—

1. Start early in the week before your class meets.

2. Overview the study. Review the table of contents and read the study introduction. Try to see how each lesson relates to the overall study.

3. Use your Bible to read and consider prayerfully the Scripture passages for the lesson. (You'll see that each writer has chosen a favorite translation for the lessons in this issue. You're free to use the Bible translation you prefer and compare it with the translation chosen for that lesson, of course.)

4. After reading all the Scripture passages in your Bible, then read the writer's comments. The comments are intended to be an aid to your study of the Bible.

5. Read the small articles—"sidebars"—in each lesson. They are intended to provide additional, enrichment information and inspiration and to encourage thought and application.

6. Try to answer for yourself the questions included in each lesson. They're intended to encourage further thought and application, and they can also be used in the class session itself.

If you're the teacher—

A. Do all of the things just mentioned, of course. As you begin the study with your class, be sure to find a way to help your class know the date on which each lesson will be studied. You might do this in one or more of the following ways:

   • In the first session of the study, briefly overview the study by identifying with your class the date on which each lesson will be studied. Lead your class to write the date in the table of contents on page 9 and on the first page of each lesson.

- Make and post a chart that indicates the date on which each lesson will be studied.

- If all of your class has e-mail, send them an e-mail with the dates the lessons will be studied.

- Provide a bookmark with the lesson dates. You may want to include information about your church and then use the bookmark as an outreach tool, too. A model for a bookmark can be downloaded from www.baptistwaypress.org on the **Adults— Bible Studies** page.

- Develop a sticker with the lesson dates, and place it on the table of contents or on the back cover.

B. Get a copy of the *Teaching Guide*, a companion piece to this *Study Guide*. The *Teaching Guide* contains additional Bible comments plus two teaching plans. The teaching plans in the *Teaching Guide* are intended to provide practical, easy-to-use teaching suggestions that will work in your class.

C. After you've studied the Bible passage, the lesson comments, and other material, use the teaching suggestions in the *Teaching Guide* to help you develop your plan for leading your class in studying each lesson.

D. Teaching resource items for use as handouts are available free at www.baptistwaypress.org.

E. Additional Bible study comments on the lessons are available online. Call 1–866–249–1799 or e-mail baptistway@texasbaptists.org to order *Adult Online Bible Commentary*. It is available only in electronic format (PDF) from our website, www.baptistwaypress.org. The price of these comments for the entire study is $6 for individuals and $25 for a group of five. A church or class that participates in our advance order program for free shipping can receive *Adult Online Bible Commentary* free. Call 1–866–249–1799 or see www.baptistwaypress.org to purchase or for information on participating in our free shipping program for the next study.

F. Additional teaching plans are also available in electronic format (PDF) by calling 1–866–249–1799. The price of these additional teaching plans for the entire study is $5 for an individual and $20 for a group of five. A church or class that participates in our advance order program for free shipping can receive *Adult Online Teaching Plans* free. Call 1–866–249–1799 or see www.baptistwaypress.org for information on participating in our free shipping program for the next study.

G. You also may want to get the enrichment teaching help that is provided on the internet by the *Baptist Standard* at www.baptiststandard.com. (Other class participants may find this information helpful, too.) The *Baptist Standard* is available online for an annual subscription rate of $10. Subscribe online at www.baptiststandard.com or call 214–630–4571. (A free ninety-day trial subscription is currently available.)

H. Enjoy leading your class in discovering the meaning of the Scripture passages and in applying these passages to their lives.

DO YOU USE A KINDLE?

This BaptistWay *Adult Bible Study Guide* plus *14 Habits of Highly Effective Disciples; Guidance for the Seasons of Life; Living Generously for Jesus' Sake; Profiles in Character; Psalms: Songs from the Heart of Faith; Jeremiah and Ezekiel: Prophets of Judgment and Hope; Amos, Hosea, Isaiah, Micah; The Gospel of Matthew; The Gospel of Mark; The Gospel of Luke: Jesus' Personal Touch; The Gospel of John: Part One; The Gospel of John: Part Two; The Book of Acts: Time to Act on Acts 1:8;* and *The Corinthian Letters: Imperatives for an Imperfect Church* are now available in a Kindle edition. The easiest way to find these materials is to search for "BaptistWay" on your Kindle or go to www.amazon.com/kindle and do a search for "BaptistWay." The Kindle edition can be studied not only on a Kindle but also on a PC, Mac, iPhone, iPad, Blackberry, or Android phone using the Kindle app available free from amazon.com/kindle.

AUDIO BIBLE STUDY LESSONS

Do you want to use your walk/run/ride, etc. time to study the Bible? Or maybe you're a college student who wants to listen to the lesson on your iPod®? Or maybe you're looking for a way to study the Bible when you just can't find time to read? Or maybe you know someone who has difficulty seeing to read even our *Large Print Study Guide*?

Then try our audio Bible study lessons, available on *Living Generously for Jesus' Sake*; *Profiles in Character*; *Amos, Hosea, Isaiah, Micah*; *The Gospel of Matthew*; *The Gospel of Mark*; *The Gospel of Luke*; *The Gospel of John: Part One*; *The Gospel of John: Part Two*; *The Book of Acts*; *The Corinthian Letters*; *Galatians and 1 & 2 Thessalonians*; and *The Letters of James and John*. For more information or to order, call 1–866–249–1799 or e-mail baptistway@texasbaptists.org. The files are downloaded from our website. You'll need an audio player that plays MP3 files (like an iPod®, but many MP3 players are available), or you can listen on a computer.

Writers for This Study Guide

Leigh Ann Powers wrote lessons one through four. This is her sixth writing assignment for BaptistWay. A mother of three, she is a graduate of Baylor University (B.S. Ed.) and Southwestern Baptist Theological Seminary (M.Div.). She attends First Baptist Church, Winters, Texas, where her husband, Heath, serves as pastor. She blogs at www.leighpowers.com.

Bob DeFoor of Harrodsburg, Kentucky, wrote lessons five through seven. Dr. DeFoor served more than forty years as pastor of churches in Kentucky and Georgia, serving the last twenty-eight prior to retirement as pastor of Harrodsburg Baptist Church. Both Bob and his wife Sandy are native Georgians, and both are graduates of Baylor University, Waco, Texas.

Phil Lineberger, writer of lessons eight through eleven, is pastor of Sugar Land Baptist Church, Sugar Land, Texas. Phil is married to Brenda, with three daughters and ten grandchildren. Dr. Lineberger has served as president of the Baptist General Convention of Texas, as a trustee for William Jewell College and Dallas Baptist University, as a regent at Baylor University, and as vice-president of the Cotton Bowl Athletic Association.

Tom Howe, who wrote lessons twelve and thirteen, is the senior pastor of Birdville Baptist Church, Haltom City, Texas. Dr. Howe is a graduate of East Texas Baptist University (B.S.), Beeson Divinity School at Samford University (M. Div.), and Southwestern Baptist Theological Seminary (D. Min.).

Letters to the Ephesians and Timothy: Guidance for the Church and Its Leaders

Studying

Letters to the Ephesians and Timothy: Guidance for the Church and Its Leaders

Why study Ephesians and 1 and 2 Timothy? For one thing, in our BaptistWay curriculum study plan, the latest previous study of Ephesians we provided was in 2008, and the latest study of 1 and 2 Timothy occurred in 2006. Now seems an appropriate time to learn from these rich resources again.[1]

Why study Ephesians and 1 and 2 Timothy *together*? One reason is that these three letters have several matters in common. One matter all three letters have in common is that all indicate that the Apostle Paul wrote them (Ephesians 1:1; 1 Timothy 1:1; 2 Timothy 1:1).

A second matter these letters have in common is that all three letters are related in some way to Ephesus, a substantial city in New Testament times in the western portion of Asia Minor (the far southwestern part of modern Turkey). It is true that in Ephesians 1:1, the words translated "in Ephesus" do not have the best manuscript support. This fact suggests that Ephesians might have been a circular letter intended for a number of churches. Even so, early on the letter came to be associated in some Christian circles of the day with Ephesus in particular.

Concerning the relation of 1 Timothy to Ephesus, 1 Timothy 1:3–4 places Timothy in Ephesus. That 2 Timothy is also related to Ephesus seems reasonable although less apparent. The only specific mention of Ephesus in 2 Timothy occurs in 2 Timothy 4:12, "Tychicus I have sent to Ephesus." That statement can be interpreted in more than one way, including that Timothy was not in Ephesus. However, it seems reasonable that the meaning of the statement is that Tychicus had carried the letter from Paul to Timothy in Ephesus[2] or perhaps that Tychicus was on his way to Timothy in Ephesus.[3] Ephesians 6:21–22 and Acts 20:4 suggest a further relationship of Tychicus to Ephesus, making the case stronger for the relation of 2 Timothy itself to Ephesus.

A third matter these letters have in common is that all three letters deal with the church (Ephesians) and the church's leaders (especially 1 and 2 Timothy but see also Ephesians 4). Perhaps this matter is the most important of the three for studying these letters in the same time frame. Studying these three letters together provides an opportunity to focus particularly on the role of the church and the church's leaders.

EPHESIANS: NOW, THROUGH THE CHURCH

Lesson 1	God's Lavish Provisions	Ephesians 1
Lesson 2	The Difference God's Love Makes	Ephesians 2:1–10
Lesson 3	The Church—Meant to Be United	Ephesians 2:11–22
Lesson 4	The Church's Mission, the Church's Needs	Ephesians 3
Lesson 5	The Church Fulfilling Its Calling	Ephesians 4:1–16
Lesson 6	Live the New Way of Christ	Ephesians 4:17—5:20
Lesson 7	Life in a Christian Household	Ephesians 5:21—6:9

1 AND 2 TIMOTHY: LEADING THE CHURCH

Lesson 8	An Example to Follow	1 Timothy 1:1–5, 12–19
Lesson 9	Qualities of Worthy Church Leaders	1 Timothy 3:1–13
Lesson 10	Train for Godliness	1 Timothy 4
Lesson 11	God or Money?	1 Timothy 6:3–19
Lesson 12	Wake Up and Keep Going	2 Timothy 1:6–14; 2:1–15
Lesson 13	Toward a Future Filled with Hope	2 Timothy 4:1–8, 16–18

NOTES

1. Unless otherwise indicated, all Scripture quotations in "Studying *Letters to the Ephesians and Timothy: Guidance for the Church and Its Leaders*" are from the New American Standard Bible (1995 edition).

2. E. Glenn Hinson, "1—2 Timothy and Titus," *The Broadman Bible Commentary,* vol. 11 (Nashville, Tennessee: Broadman Press, 1971), 358.

3. A.T. Robertson, *Word Pictures in the New Testament,* vol. IV (Nashville, Tennessee: Broadman Press, 1931), 632.

Introducing

EPHESIANS: Now, Through the Church

Ephesus was a leading city in the Roman province of Asia Minor, which geographically is part of modern-day Turkey. Many Bible students, however, consider Paul's Letter to the Ephesians to have been intended for the church as a whole, not just the church at Ephesus specifically. One reason for this, as mentioned in "Studying Letters to the Ephesians and Timothy," is that in Ephesians 1:1, the words translated "in Ephesus" do not have the best manusript support.

The Letter to the Ephesians is rich in content. It begins with a broad, majestic view of what God has done in Christ, making special application to what this means for the church (Ephesians 1—3). It continues with directions for how the church is to live in the real world in response to what God has done (Eph. 4—6).

In the letter's first-century context, one of its great concerns was helping people of Gentile and Jewish background in the church realize that through God's grace God in Christ "broke down the barrier of the dividing wall, by abolishing in his flesh the enmity" that separated people (2:14).[1] That's still good news in our broken world in which so many barriers between people continue to exist. These barriers divide even the church so that its sharing of the good news is suspect. If community cannot exist in the church, how can the church's communication of the message of reconciliation mean anything? What the church does can block and distort what it says. Even so, the message of Ephesians is that God in Christ can bring reconciliation between people. Even those who like the Gentiles once were "strangers to the covenants of promise" (2:11) can now be "fellow citizens with the saints, and . . . of God's household" (2:19).

The mission of the church now is to live and share this glorious message of what God has done in Christ and what it means. Ephesians reminds us that God has given the church an assignment larger than we often think: "that the manifold wisdom of God might now be made known through the church to the rulers and the authorities in the heavenly places" (3:10). In addition to the wide-ranging nature of this mission, Ephesians further asserts the place of the church in God's plan by applying to the church the expression "the body of Christ" (1:22–23; 4:13–16).[2]

As we see such lofty expressions applied to the church, should we not be challenged to consider how our local churches, which often seem so limited and provincial (or worse), can live up to them, or at least come nearer to them? How can the church that has an earthly mailing address and of which you are a member truly be "the body of Christ" and fulfill the mission of making known "the manifold wisdom of God"?

EPHESIANS: NOW, THROUGH THE CHURCH

Lesson 1	God's Lavish Provisions	Ephesians 1
Lesson 2	The Difference God's Love Makes	Ephesian 2:1–10
Lesson 3	The Church—Meant to Be United	Ephesians 2:11–22
Lesson 4	The Church's Mission, the Church's Needs	Ephesians 3
Lesson 5	The Church Fulfilling Its Calling	Ephesians 4:1–16
Lesson 6	Live the New Way of Christ	Ephesians 4:17—5:20
Lesson 7	Life in a Christian Household	Ephesians 5:21—6:9

Additional Resources for Studying Ephesians:[3]

F.F. Bruce. *Colossians, Philemon, and Ephesians.* New International Commentary on the New Testament. Grand Rapids, Michigan: Eerdmans Publishing Company, 1984.

Lewis R. Donelson, *Colossians, Ephesians, 1 and 2 Timothy and Titus.* Westminster Bible Companion. Louisville, Kentucky, Westminster John Knox Press, 1996.

Craig S. Keener. *IVP Bible Background Commentary: New Testament.* Downers Grove, Illinois: InterVarsity Press, 1993.

Andrew T. Lincoln. *Ephesians.* Word Biblical Commentary. Volume 42. Dallas, Texas: Word Books, Publisher, 1990.

Tremper Longman III and David E. Garland, general editors. *The Expositor's Bible Commentary, Revised Edition*, Volume 12. Grand Rapids, Michigan, Zondervan, 2006.

Ralph P. Martin. "Ephesians." *The Broadman Bible Commentary.* Volume 11. Nashville, Tennessee: Broadman Press, 1971.

Ralph P. Martin. *Ephesians, Colossians, Philemon.* Interpretation: A Bible Commentary for Teaching and Preaching. Atlanta: John Knox Press, 1991.

Pheme Perkins. "The Letter to the Ephesians." *The New Interpreter's Bible.* Volume XI. Nashville, Tennessee: Abingdon Press, 2000.

A.T. Robertson. *Word Pictures in the New Testament.* Volume IV. Nashville, Tennessee: Broadman Press, 1931.

Thomas B. Slater. *Ephesians.* Smyth & Helwys Bible Commentary. Macon, Georgia: Smyth & Helwys Publishing, Inc., 2012.

Malcolm O. Tolbert. *Ephesians: God's New People.* Nashville, Tennessee: Convention Press, 1979.

NOTES

1. Unless otherwise indicated, all Scripture quotations in "Introducing Ephesians: Now, Through the Church" are from the New American Standard Bible (1995 edition).

2. See also Romans 12:3–8; 1 Corinthians 12:12–31; Colossians 1:18.

3. Listing a book does not imply full agreement by the writers or BAPTISTWAY PRESS® with all of its comments.

MAIN IDEA

God has lavishly and graciously provided salvation through Christ, who is Lord over all.

QUESTION TO EXPLORE

Why do we sometimes think of church as mere duty and obligation—or optional—when God has so lavishly provided salvation for us?

STUDY AIM

To describe God's lavish provisions of salvation through Christ

QUICK READ

God has showered his people with lavish grace so that we can bring glory to him.

LESSON ONE
God's Lavish Provisions

When my husband and I were in seminary, we moved into our small apartment in the middle of a hot July weekend. That first Sunday evening we wanted to go to church. We weren't sure where to go, but we had seen a church across the street from our apartment and decided to go there for at least one service.

We slipped in and sat in back, finding familiar comfort in the hymns and Scripture reading. When the service was over, we were warmly welcomed by a crowd of people, including several couples who invited us to join them for a baked potato fellowship. Something in the simple, genuine welcome made it clear that this was where God wanted us to be.

Gambrell Street Baptist was a good congregation for two young seminary students to find their place. So many of the pews were filled by pastors and missionaries who were willing to share their experiences with us. It was a place where we could serve, learn, and worship, and a place where we were known. When I think about the blessings of Christian community, the fellowship we enjoyed at that church stands out to me as how church should be.

Church should be a place of blessing, but sometimes it winds up feeling more like an obligation. In the midst of soccer games and commutes, doctor's bills and carpool lanes, church can sometimes seem like one more thing on the to-do list—something that keeps us from sleeping in instead of a place where we meet God and God's people. God meant for church to be more than that. Church should be a place where we experience the blessings of salvation together with the community of faith and channel those blessings to a waiting world.[1]

EPHESIANS 1

[1] Paul, an apostle of Christ Jesus by the will of God, To the saints in Ephesus, the faithful in Christ Jesus: [2] Grace and peace to you from God our Father and the Lord Jesus Christ.

[3] Praise be to the God and Father of our Lord Jesus Christ, who has blessed us in the heavenly realms with every spiritual blessing in Christ. [4] For he chose us in him before the creation of the world to be holy and blameless in his sight. In love [5] he predestined us to be adopted as his sons through Jesus Christ, in accordance with his pleasure and will— [6] to the praise of his glorious grace,

which he has freely given us in the One he loves. [7] In him we have redemption through his blood, the forgiveness of sins, in accordance with the riches of God's grace [8] that he lavished on us with all wisdom and understanding. [9] And he made known to us the mystery of his will according to his good pleasure, which he purposed in Christ, [10] to be put into effect when the times will have reached their fulfillment—to bring all things in heaven and on earth together under one head, even Christ. [11] In him we were also chosen, having been predestined according to the plan of him who works out everything in conformity with the purpose of his will, [12] in order that we, who were the first to hope in Christ, might be for the praise of his glory. [13] And you also were included in Christ when you heard the word of truth, the gospel of your salvation. Having believed, you were marked in him with a seal, the promised Holy Spirit, [14] who is a deposit guaranteeing our inheritance until the redemption of those who are God's possession—to the praise of his glory.

[15] For this reason, ever since I heard about your faith in the Lord Jesus and your love for all the saints, [16] I have not stopped giving thanks for you, remembering you in my prayers. [17] I keep asking that the God of our Lord Jesus Christ, the glorious Father, may give you the Spirit of wisdom and revelation, so that you may know him better. [18] I pray also that the eyes of your heart may be enlightened in order that you may know the hope to which he has called you, the riches of his glorious inheritance in the saints, [19] and his incomparably great power for us who believe. That power is like the working of his mighty strength, [20] which he exerted in Christ when he raised him from the dead and seated him at his right hand in the heavenly realms, [21] far above all rule and authority, power and dominion, and every title that can be given, not only in the present age but also in the one to come. [22] And God placed all things under his feet and appointed him to be head over everything for the church, [23] which is his body, the fullness of him who fills everything in every way.

We Are Blessed (1:1–10)

Paul often opened his letters with a thanksgiving. In Ephesians, Paul began with a long and complicated blessing. Paul praised God for blessing his people and then listed God's lavish blessings.

The first year my husband and I were married we set aside a few dollars each month so we could buy presents for each other. That first Christmas Heath was determined to make our little Christmas budget stretch as far as he could, and so he set his alarm to go off before dawn and set out to brave the mall. When Christmas came I couldn't believe everything he had managed to come up with. He lavished his love on me.

God loves us like that. He doesn't hold anything back; he isn't stingy. Instead, God lavishes his blessings on us. We experience God's blessings in Christ. These spiritual blessings aren't saved up for us to experience later. God has already poured them out on us from his home in the "heavenly realms" (Ephesians 1:3). We experience God's blessings as we pursue intimacy with him—an intimacy made available through Christ's sacrifice for us.

RELIGIOUS LIFE IN EPHESUS

Ephesus was a melting pot of religious pluralism. Although the city was known for the worship of Artemis, the city was home to as many as fifty other gods and goddesses. The city was also known as a center for magic and the occult (Acts 19:13–20). The practice of magic was built on the belief that good and evil spirits were involved in almost every area of life. Magicians believed that they could harness the power of these spirits through rituals, magic spells, and incantations. Many also believed that the stars and planets had the power to control their fate and that their lives could be determined by the movement of the stars. One of the things that drew some people to worship Artemis was that they believed that as the queen of heaven she had the power to change fate. It was important for the Ephesians to understand that God's power far surpassed any other spiritual power and that it was God, not the stars and planets, who set the course of history.[3]

Foremost among God's blessings is that God chose us "before the creation of the world" (Eph. 1:4). God knew what choosing us would mean. Revelation tells us that Christ "was slain from the creation of the world" (Revelation 13:8). Before creation began, God saw it all: the garden, the serpent, and the fall. He knew the mess a fallen humanity would make of this world. He saw us in our sin; he saw the wars, the famines, the lies, the hate, and the ones who would mock his name. Over it all, God saw the cross: the only possible path to redeem humanity from our slavery to sin. God knew the price and chose us anyway.

God chose us, but he also chose us for a purpose: "to be holy and blameless in his sight" (Eph. 1:4). "Blameless" means to be free from blemish or fault. Holiness means *set apart, or reflecting the character of God*. God lovingly predestined us not to sin's slavery but to adoption as sons and daughters of God. It pleased God to call us his own. God's grace is his good and loving intentions toward us revealed in Christ.

God also blessed us by redeeming us from our slavery to sin. "Redemption" means *to be purchased back*. The price of our freedom was the blood of Christ. God blesses us with full and complete "forgiveness"—a forgiveness in agreement "with the riches of God's grace that he lavished on us" (1:7).

Although I know what the Bible says about forgiveness, I am often tempted to put limits on my forgiveness of others. At other times I think that my failures disqualify me from God's favor. The truth is that we cannot out-sin the grace of God. There is no sin so great that God cannot forgive and redeem. The weight of our sin is overwhelmed by the wealth of God's lavish grace.

God chose us, forgave us, and blessed us by revealing his will to us. In God's wisdom and understanding, God revealed to us "the mystery of his will" (1:9). When Paul spoke of the mystery of God's will, he was not talking about a problem that has to be solved, like the plot of an Agatha Christie novel. In Paul's letters, a "mystery" describes something that was once hidden and now made known. God's plan for salvation in Christ was hidden from the priests and prophets but is now revealed to the church.

Yet God's plan is not limited to our redemption. God's redemptive plan looks forward to a day at the fullness of time when all creation is brought into its rightful place under the authority of Christ. Our unity in the church is a foretaste of the day when all of the created order will be united in submission to the Lordship of Christ (Romans 8:19–21).

We Are Chosen (1:11–14)

God's blessings are made available to us in our unity and submission with Christ. From the beginning God chose us and gave us an eternal destiny in accordance with his will. Our destinies are not determined by the stars, fate, genetics, or chance. Rather, our future is guided by a loving God who works to see that all things ultimately conform to the purpose of his will. This does not mean that everything that happens to us is a part of God's will but that God is constantly at work to bring our lives into conformity with his redemptive purposes.

God chose us for a purpose: to praise his glory (Eph. 1:11–12). God's glory shines in our brokenness made whole. When God redeems and transforms saints into sinners, God demonstrates his power as a God of redemption and grace. Both the Jews, "the first to hope in Christ," and the Gentiles, "you also," were included in Christ. No longer separate, Jew and Gentile were united together in the body of Christ.

We also find our place in the community of grace. Salvation is not just for those whose parents taught them to toddle through the church doors as soon as they could walk. It's for all of us. Male and female, mechanics and millionaires, people of all races—all are included in Christ when they hear and believe the good news of our salvation.

When we believed, God marked us with the seal of the Holy Spirit. In the New Testament world a seal was the most common way to express ownership. Valuables, documents, and even slaves or livestock were marked with seals.[2] The Holy Spirit is a "seal" identifying us as God's own possession, purchased by Christ's blood.

The Holy Spirit is also a "deposit" that guarantees our future inheritance. When we buy a home, we have to put down a down payment that allows us to take ownership and guarantees the transaction will be completed. Similarly, the Holy Spirit's presence in our lives is a deposit of the eternal inheritance we will ultimately receive in the presence of God. The Spirit is God's guarantee that God will keep his promises and finish the redemptive work he has already begun.

HOW TO APPLY THIS LESSON

- Plan a fellowship or worship event together with a congregation from a different language group. Celebrate the unity you have together in Christ.
- Write out your testimony. How has God redeemed and blessed you?
- Put Paul's prayer in Ephesians 1:15–23 in your own words. Pray this prayer for your church.

We Are Known (1:15–23)

After finishing his lengthy blessing, Paul turned to a prayer for the Ephesian church. Paul had heard about the church's faith in God and love for all God's people. Paul's thankfulness for the church's faithfulness overflowed into a prayer of blessing on the congregation.

Paul's first concern was that the church would know God better. For that reason he prayed that they might have a "Spirit of wisdom and revelation"—either a reference to the Holy Spirit or a prayer that they would grow in wisdom and understanding of God (1:17). Paul's intent wasn't just academic knowledge. *Knowing* in the Bible is almost always experiential. Paul's prayer was that they know God intimately—the kind of intimacy gained only through creating your personal history with God.

To that end, Paul prayed that "the eyes of your heart may be enlightened" (1:18). His prayer was that the church would gain supernatural insight and understanding that would help them see and understand what God was doing in and through them.

One of the reasons Paul wanted the church to grow in spiritual insight was so that they would understand "the riches of his glorious inheritance in the saints" (1:18). God has chosen the church for his own inheritance. We are valuable and precious to God.

Our experiences of church don't always match up with the spiritual reality. Sometimes what was meant to be a place of healing becomes a place of wounding. Sometimes church can feel like one more item on the to do list. But it was meant to be more. If God himself regards the church as valuable and precious, shouldn't we?

Paul also wants us to understand God's "incomparably great power for us who believe" (1:19). The same power that raised Jesus Christ from the dead is available to us through the Holy Spirit. God raised Christ from the dead and put him in authority over every human and spiritual power in heaven and earth—not only now but for all of eternity. Christ is head over all things, and we—his church—are the body of Christ. Christ's life and power fills the church, and we fill the world with the glory of God as we share the good news of God's redeeming work in Christ. We should not fear that we are too small or lack the resources for the task. God's mighty strength is available to us.

Implications and Actions

God intended the church to be a demonstration of his glory and power, a foretaste of what it looks like to live in the kingdom of God. Sometimes our experience of church falls short of God's design. Church was meant to be a place of healing, but it can become a place of wounding. Sometimes we mistake activity for God's presence and assume a full calendar of events is a sign of God's favor. At other times we make the mistake of thinking it's all about us—that church is meant to cater to our taste preferences rather to celebrate God's lavish grace.

Church is meant to be more than that. When we come together as the community of the redeemed, we celebrate God's work in us and anticipate his coming. We offer a feast of grace to those most hungry for the good news of salvation. We become the hands and feet of Christ, filling the earth with his glory as we spread out taking the gospel to the nations and living it among them. Church is not duty or obligation but a chance to celebrate and participate in God's redemptive work.

QUESTIONS

1. How have you experienced God's lavish blessings through the church?

2. Why do we sometimes see church as obligation or optional? How does understanding God's lavish grace affect your views of church?

3. How does your church show the glory of God to the world?

4. How has your personal history with God helped you grow in the knowledge of God?

NOTES

1. Unless otherwise indicated, all Scripture quotations in lessons 1–13 are from the New International Version (1984 edition).

2. Clinton E. Arnold, "Ephesians," *Zondervan Illustrated Bible Backgrounds Commentary*, vol. 3 (Grand Rapids: Zondervan, 2002), 308–309.

3. Arnold, 302–303, 306.

MAIN IDEA

Only God's mercy, grace, and love, and not our goodness, make the difference in our experience of church and indeed of all of life.

QUESTION TO EXPLORE

What place does God's mercy, grace, and love have in your present experience of church and indeed of all of life?

STUDY AIM

To describe the difference God's mercy, grace, and love make for life now and forever

QUICK READ

God's mercy, grace, and love toward us in Christ Jesus take us from death to life and give us an eternal purpose.

LESSON TWO
The Difference God's Love Makes

When I was a child my uncle and cousins went out to the deer woods to hunt every fall. One year my father took me to visit their deer camp. We walked through the woods and sat in one of the deer blinds watching for deer. As we headed back to camp, my uncle had hung one of the deer he had shot from a tree. My father wanted to get a picture of me next to the deer. I obediently stood next to the deer and let him snap my picture. As I turned back around a gust of wind caught the deer and spun it toward me. I found myself looking straight into the gutted carcass of the deer.

It was not a pleasant moment for me. This image from my childhood has stood out in my mind when I think of death. Death is final, permanent, and impartial. Paul chose the image of death to describe our condition apart from Christ.

EPHESIANS 2:1–10

[1] As for you, you were dead in your transgressions and sins, [2] in which you used to live when you followed the ways of this world and of the ruler of the kingdom of the air, the spirit who is now at work in those who are disobedient. [3] All of us also lived among them at one time, gratifying the cravings of our sinful nature and following its desires and thoughts. Like the rest, we were by nature objects of wrath. [4] But because of his great love for us, God, who is rich in mercy, [5] made us alive with Christ even when we were dead in transgressions—it is by grace you have been saved. [6] And God raised us up with Christ and seated us with him in the heavenly realms in Christ Jesus, [7] in order that in the coming ages he might show the incomparable riches of his grace, expressed in his kindness to us in Christ Jesus. [8] For it is by grace you have been saved, through faith—and this not from yourselves, it is the gift of God— [9] not by works, so that no one can boast. [10] For we are God's workmanship, created in Christ Jesus to do good works, which God prepared in advance for us to do.

Dead in Sin (2:1–3)

Apart from God we were dead in our sin. Sin results in both physical and spiritual death. Death entered the world through Adam's sin,[1] and our sin separates us from God. Apart from God there is no spiritual life in us. Without Christ, we are all dead men walking.

The "we" and "you" pronouns Paul used in this section most likely refer to Jews and Gentiles in the Ephesian church, but the plural nature of these pronouns also reminds us that no one is exempt. All of us were dead in our sins apart from Christ. Before we followed Christ we followed the pattern set by our world and the "ruler of the kingdom of the air," Satan (Ephesians 2:2). It's a disturbing thought. We like to see ourselves as *not that bad*. Sure, we've sinned, but even apart from Christ we had a certain moral code. The truth is that there is no middle ground. Satan's rebellion against God means that anything other than allegiance to Christ is a victory for Satan. Satan works in those who are disobedient to make sure they stay that way. He uses any technique at his disposal—lies, spiritual apathy, fear, or distraction—to keep people from following God. Satan desires to keep us bound in our spiritual death, and before we followed Christ we all followed him (Eph. 2:2).

Self-centeredness is one characteristic of spiritual death (2:3). The Book of James says that temptation arises from our desires that war within us (James 1:14). Apart from Christ, our natural tendency is to indulge our own cravings and desires.

We sin because it feels good to us. It feels good to give the person who offended us a piece of our mind. It feels right to spend our money on ourselves without thinking of others. It's only natural to linger over the erotic novel or photograph. When relationships become more work than fun, it seems right to us to end the relationship to escape the pain. It's enjoyable to laugh at the sitcom or enjoy the beat of the song without thinking about the deeper messages media conveys. At its core, sin puts us on the throne of our own kingdoms. We gratify our own desires and cravings because it pleases the only ruler that counts: ourselves. Setting ourselves up as ruler over our own lives puts us in direct rebellion against God.

In our rebellion against God we were deserving of God's wrath (Eph. 2:3). We should not equate the wrath of God with human anger. In the Bible God's wrath is synonymous with judgment. God's holiness means that God is perfect in his love, but it also means that God is perfect in his judgment. For God not to stand in opposition to sin would be contrary to the holy nature and character of God. Apart from God, our default setting is rebellion against God. Our natural tendency to sin means that we all deserve God's judgment. Again, Paul used a plural pronoun here. There are no exemptions. No matter how upstanding or righteous we may appear to be on our own, we all have sinned. All of us deserve death.

But God (2:4–7)

We were dead in sin, but God loved us anyway. When a heart attack victim flatlines, the person is completely at the mercy of the doctors and nurses to revive him. Dead people can't help themselves. Similarly, we are powerless to save ourselves. We were sinners, but God showed us mercy. We were in bondage, but God set us free. We were unlovable, but God loved us anyway. We were dead, but God gave us life.

B.H. CARROLL

Benajah Harvey (B.H.) Carroll was the son of a bivocational pastor, but he did not automatically adopt his family's devout faith. Carroll considered himself an "infidel" for many years. He believed in God but doubted that the Bible was the word of God, that miracles were real, and that Jesus was divine. After the failure of his first marriage and the death of his father, B.H. Carroll severed his ties to the church and rejected any hope of Christianity. He vowed never to enter another church.

Carroll was gravely wounded during the Civil War. In the aftermath of the war and the economic crisis of Reconstruction, Carroll was finally forced to admit the secular philosophy he had adopted provided no real hope or solutions. In 1865 Carroll's mother persuaded him to go to a Methodist camp meeting. Carroll wasn't impressed by the service, but he was gripped by the minister's plea to make a "practical, experiential test" of faith. Later Carroll experienced a vision that spurred his memory of Jesus' call to "come unto me." Carroll accepted God's call to preach and was soon baptized. The former "infidel" went on to write eighteen volumes of sermons, influence Texas Baptists to form the Baptist General Convention of Texas, serve as president of the trustees for Baylor University for more than twenty years, and help found Southwestern Baptist Theological Seminary.[2]

God's grace toward us says nothing about our worth and everything about God's character. Only a God who is perfect in love could love the unlovable. Because God is rich in mercy, God showed us grace by sending Christ. God didn't just pardon our sin; God gave us more than we could have ever dared ask or think by sending Christ. Jesus' death and resurrection took us from death to life. His sacrifice paid a debt we could never have hoped to repay. God didn't just settle for erasing our sin. He gave us new life by uniting us with Christ. Although we were in rebellion against God, we now share in Christ's victory over sin and death. God's grace means we are no longer slaves to sin; we have the freedom to live in obedience to God. We were saved for a purpose. God didn't redeem us so we could live like trembling captives. He did all this so that in the ages of eternity to come he might show us "the incomparable riches of his grace," displayed in the kindness God demonstrated in sending Jesus to die for us. We deserved God's wrath, but instead God showed us mercy.

Saved by Grace (2:8–10)

The one thing most world religions have in common is that at the end of the day what happens after death depends on being a good person. If you have followed the rules and lived morally as defined by that religion, all will go well with you in the afterlife. Christianity is the exception to that rule.

What Ephesians explicitly teaches us is that our salvation does not depend on our own effort. "For it is by grace you have been saved, through faith —and this not from yourselves, it is the gift of God—not by works, so that no one can boast" (Eph. 2:8). Our own goodness is nothing compared to God's holiness. God cannot accept sin into his presence. Every lying word, every vengeful thought, and every selfish action adds to the weight of sin that separates us from a holy God. All are guilty, and all stand condemned.

But there is good news! God graciously sent his Son, Jesus, to pay the penalty for our sin. The price of sin is death, and God's perfect justice demanded that it be paid. God's perfect love compelled God himself to take our place in the person of God's own Son, Jesus Christ. We bring nothing to the table. Jesus' sacrifice was sufficient to pay the penalty for

CASE STUDY

Jamie accepted Christ when she was fifteen. As an adult she struggles to balance the demands of family, work, and church. She teaches Sunday School, sings in the choir, leads the Wednesday night children's activity, and coordinates the women's ministry. You've noticed for several weeks that she seems not quite herself, and you ask her how she's doing. Jamie breaks down in tears and confesses that she's exhausted. She knows she's doing too much but is afraid to drop anything because she fears letting people down. "I just want to please God," she says. What would you tell Jamie?

our sins, once and for all. In Jesus' death, God gave us more than we could have ever deserved. He gave us grace.

Salvation is the free gift of our gracious God. We simply receive it by calling on the name of Jesus. We do this when we acknowledge our own sin, ask God's forgiveness, and commit ourselves to following Jesus Christ as Lord. Following Christ as Lord means that we remove ourselves from the throne of our own lives and surrender our will to the rightful rule of Jesus Christ. Instead of serving our own selfish desires, we serve the God who in Christ gave his life for us. We receive this gift by faith—believing that what God has promised God will do. Even the faith by which we receive salvation does not come from ourselves but from God. No one comes to God unless God has first worked to draw the person to himself (John 6:44).

We are saved for a purpose. God displays his glory by bringing wholeness from the brokenness of our sin. We are God's workmanship, his masterpieces, declaring to the world that our God is a God who redeems. We are created in him to do good works that God has prepared for us from the beginning. No matter where we have been or what we have done, the blood of Christ declares us whole. There is no sin so great that God cannot forgive, no debt so great that it outweighs the wealth of God's grace.

Implications and Actions

How should we live in light of this great grace we have received? The only appropriate responses well up out of thanksgiving to God for God's marvelous grace. When we understand that salvation depends entirely on God's goodness and not our own, such an understanding should infuse our lives with thankful love. We serve God not because we are trying to earn God's favor, but out of gratitude to the God whose great mercy, grace, and love has made us whole.

That grateful love should also overflow into how we treat others. We cannot accept God's gracious forgiveness for ourselves and then demand others earn our favor. Jesus' death was sufficient to pay the price for all sin—both the sins we commit and those others commit against us. Salvation is a free gift offered to all, and we should offer it freely.

Similarly, we should treat others in the church as the redeemed sons and daughters of God. Too often in the church we let petty conflicts divide us. The color of the carpet, the style of worship music, and who said what to whom at the football game should not be fighting matters for the children of God.

God has extended grace, mercy, and love to us. We should extend that same grace, mercy, and love to others—beginning with our church family. Jesus said that the world would know us by our love. Let us love one another so well that the world recognizes us as a people who have been with God.

QUESTIONS

1. How would you describe spiritual death?

2. Why do you think we sometimes try to excuse or explain away our own sinfulness?

3. What impact should knowing we are saved by the grace of God have on how we live? on how we treat others?

4. Even though we know we are saved by God's grace, why do we sometimes still act as if we have to earn God's favor?

5. How should God's mercy, grace, and love affect our experience of church?

NOTES

1. See Genesis 3:22–23; Romans 5:12.

2. James Spivey, "Benajah Harvey Carroll," Timothy George and David Dockery, eds., *Theologians of the Baptist Tradition* [Kindle edition] (Nashville: Broadman and Holman, 2001).

FOCAL TEXT
Ephesians 2:11–22

BACKGROUND
Ephesians 2:11–22

MAIN IDEA
God in Christ has made it possible for a church composed of people who formerly disagreed with, disliked, and even hated one another to be united through Christ's work on behalf of all of them.

QUESTION TO EXPLORE
If the unity of Christians is so important, why has the church as a whole never had it, why is it so hard to have even in a local church, and how can it be attained?

STUDY AIM
To describe the unity God has made possible in Christ and identify how we can move toward that unity today, beginning with my own church

QUICK READ
Through Jesus, God tears down the walls that divide us and unites us into a new community: the people of God, his church.

LESSON THREE
The Church— Meant to Be United

The fight started the Sunday the hymnals were put in the pews. The new hymnals had sat on a display table in the church foyer for more than a year to encourage church members to donate funds. The congregation had plenty of time to inspect them and raise questions, but it wasn't until after the new hymnals had been purchased and placed in the pews that anyone spoke out. The choir director had committed a grievous sin in the eyes of a few church members: purchasing a hymnal different from the traditional hymnal the church had used for so long. It was not our congregation's best hour.

Of course, it wasn't really about the hymnals. Like the color of the carpet, the wording on the church bulletin, or the length of the pastor's sermons, the hymnals were only an excuse to bring deeper feelings and resentments to the fore. It's not about the carpet. It's about control. It's not about being first in line at the buffet. It's about fearing change. It's not the hymnals; it's about being heard.

When you think about it, church conflict seems almost inevitable. We naturally flock to places where we can associate with people like ourselves. Where else are we asked to gather with people from different family traditions, social classes, ethnic groups, educational backgrounds, genders, passions, and generations, and still get along other than the church? No wonder so many church plants get started through church splits.

Yet Christ expects more of us than this. In his death Christ tore down the walls that divide us and built us together into a single family of faith. In Jesus we can experience the blessings of unity in the church.

EPHESIANS 2:11–22

11 Therefore, remember that formerly you who are Gentiles by birth and called "uncircumcised" by those who call themselves "the circumcision" (that done in the body by the hands of men)— 12 remember that at that time you were separate from Christ, excluded from citizenship in Israel and foreigners to the covenants of the promise, without hope and without God in the world. 13 But now in Christ Jesus you who once were far away have been brought near through the blood of Christ. 14 For he himself is our peace, who has made the two one and has destroyed the barrier,

the dividing wall of hostility, [15] by abolishing in his flesh the law with its commandments and regulations. His purpose was to create in himself one new man out of the two, thus making peace, [16] and in this one body to reconcile both of them to God through the cross, by which he put to death their hostility. [17] He came and preached peace to you who were far away and peace to those who were near. [18] For through him we both have access to the Father by one Spirit. [19] Consequently, you are no longer foreigners and aliens, but fellow citizens with God's people and members of God's household, [20] built on the foundation of the apostles and prophets, with Christ Jesus himself as the chief cornerstone. [21] In him the whole building is joined together and rises to become a holy temple in the Lord. [22] And in him you too are being built together to become a dwelling in which God lives by his Spirit.

Those Who Are Far Away Now Brought Near (2:11–13)

I think we often gloss over or fail to understand the magnitude of the miracle God accomplished in uniting Jews and Gentiles into a single church. And yet, we don't have to think back any further than our country's own racial history to begin to understand. It wasn't so long ago that a black man could be beaten for daring to sit in the "white's only" portion of a lunch counter, or that Jackie Robinson got death threats for daring to be the first black man to play baseball in the major leagues. Remembering our tragic legacy of segregation helps us understand the depth of division that existed between Jews and Gentiles in the first century.

Jews looked down on Gentiles, the "uncircumcised." Jewish men took pride in their circumcision as a physical sign that they were members of God's covenant community. Jews regarded Gentiles as outsiders and foreigners. The only way a Gentile could become a member of the community was to become Jewish. Men had to submit to circumcision and follow the law. There was a clear and visible separation, and the Jews were proud of it.

Paul reminded Gentile believers of where they stood before knowing Christ. Without Christ they had no access to the community of faith; they were "excluded from citizenship in Israel" by virtue of their birth (Ephesians 2:12). They were foreigners who were cut off from the covenant God had made with Abraham and his descendants that Jews claimed as their heritage. Gentiles had no place in the divine promise and no hope of the coming Messiah. They were "without God." Although the Gentiles worshiped many gods, they were without knowledge of the true God. They were excluded and separated, with no hope of ever coming near to God.

Jesus changed everything. "But now in Christ you who were once far away have been brought near by the blood of Christ" (Eph. 2:13). The prophets had promised a day when God would preach peace to those both far and near (Isaiah 57:19). That promise was fulfilled in Christ. Although the Gentiles had once been "far away," God had brought them near to himself through the blood of Christ. It wasn't enough to redeem only the Jews. God's plans had always included salvation for the entire world. All peoples were brought near to God by the blood of Christ.

Christ Is Our Peace (2:14–18)

In his death Jesus tore down the dividing wall between Jew and Gentile. Gentiles were permitted access into the outer courts of the Jerusalem temple—but only the outer court. A four-foot high wall separated the court of the Gentiles from the inner court. The Jewish historian Josephus reported that thirteen signs were positioned at intervals around the barrier, warning Gentiles not to go any further. Archeologists have found two of these signs. Their Greek and Latin inscriptions warn that any "foreigner" who goes past the barrier "will have himself to blame for his subsequent death."[1] The image of that barrier might have been fresh in Paul's mind. Paul wrote Ephesians from prison. The reason for his imprisonment was that the Jews had falsely accused Paul of taking a Gentile man, Trophimus, with him into the temple (Acts 21:28–29).

The temple wall was only an image of the real barrier, however. The real barrier between Jews and Gentiles was the Jewish law. The law defined Jewish existence. It governed every part of Jewish life. The food they ate, the clothes they wore, the festivals they celebrated, the way they conducted business, and even the way they washed the cups were all defined by the law. Jews celebrated the law for helping them maintain purity and keeping them separate from the nations around them. It certainly did that. Jews would not even enter the home of a Gentile because doing so would make them unclean. The law even caused division in the church. One of the earliest church conflicts broke out because Peter and other prominent Jewish believers would not eat with Gentile Christians at Antioch (Galatians 2:11–14).

Jesus tore down the wall and made peace. Jesus abolished the law, not as a tool to help us understand God's law and character, but as a list of regulations that we have to fulfill. We don't come to God by successfully keeping the rules; we come to God by grace through faith in Jesus Christ. Jesus became our peace (Isaiah 9:6; 53:5). Through the cross Jesus combined Jew and Gentile into one new family defined not by blood but by faith (Eph. 2:15). In his death Jesus put hostility itself to death—both the hostility between us and God and the hostility we have toward one another. There was to be no more separation between Jew and Gentile in the body of Christ. The same should be true for us.

Fellow Citizens (2:19–22)

Two years ago we welcomed our new sister-in-law into our family. She's from Southeast Asia, which meant that before she and my brother-in-law could get married they had to go through government channels in two countries. In the process she got her green card and permanent

CASE STUDY

The new pastor of FBC Small Town was caught off guard when the business meeting erupted into a war zone over what should have been a minor matter. The next day he learned that several years ago a nephew of the Austin family had complained about a youth pastor who was a member of the Brown family. Eventually the youth pastor was forced to resign. The Browns blamed the Austins, and the two families had barely tolerated each other since. Other members of the church felt forced to take sides. What advice would you give this congregation?

residency in the United States. She lives and works here, but she is without the full rights and privileges of a citizen.

It was similar in ancient Rome. Citizens of Rome had certain legal protections. It was illegal for Roman citizens to be crucified, and Roman citizens could not be beaten without due process (Acts 16:37–39). Male Roman citizens could vote, legally marry, and be considered the heads of their households. Citizenship could be bought or received by birth, but not every person born in Rome was a Roman citizen. There were also levels of citizenship, each with its own level of corresponding rights.

This is not the way of the kingdom of God. Jew and Gentile both have access to God by the same Spirit. Together all of us are built into one family and household of faith. There are no second-class saints. We are all fellow-citizens of the kingdom.

Paul switched from the kingdom metaphor to speak of the church as a spiritual building. The church is founded on the proclamation of Christ by the apostles and prophets, with Christ Jesus himself as the cornerstone. The cornerstone was the foundation stone used to determine the shape and lie of the entire building. The church is founded on the pattern set by Jesus.

In the Old Testament, God's Spirit dwelt within the temple. The temple was at the center of Jewish faith; it was the place where God's glory dwelt and where people went to do business with God. In the New Testament, the temple is replaced by the church. God's Spirit no longer dwells in walls of stone but in the hearts and souls of the redeemed. It is a corporate experience. We speak of *asking Jesus into our individual hearts*, and that is true, but the Bible also makes it clear that we experience the blessings of salvation together. We are united together in our love and pursuit of Christ. Drawing closer to Jesus draws us closer to one another as well. Our unity with one another is rooted and grounded in our unity with Christ.

Implications and Actions

The distinction between Jew and Gentile may not resonate with us today as much as it did in the first century, certainly not in the same manner today as then. Even so, we have found other ways of dividing. We splinter among age groups and economic strata. We divide ourselves by race and gender. We separate ourselves into families, factions, and cliques. We draw lines between those who have always been here and those who are still learning to speak the language of faith. We focus on our differences instead of the One who unites us.

Christ's death tore down the dividing wall between Jew and Gentile. His death destroyed the walls that divide us as well. We find unity in our worship of a common Savior and Lord. We are united in proclaiming Christ together and in loving one another so well that the world recognizes God's love in us. When we come together in faith, the risen Christ dwells in our midst. We can move toward unity by practicing forgiveness and reconciliation. We can focus on pursuing Christ together, spurring one another on to growth. We can pray for one another, serve one another, and choose to yield in love instead of clinging to our own rights in pride. What could God accomplish through a united church?

QUESTIONS

1. Why is unity so often a challenge for the church? How does lack of unity impact our witness?

2. We say that all are welcome in our church, but do we mean it? What are some of the unconscious or unspoken barriers that may keep people from feeling fully welcome in your church?

3. If we as the church are "being built together to become a dwelling in which God lives by his Spirit" (Eph. 2:22), how should that impact our lives together as the people of God? How is our church putting that spiritual reality into practice?

4. Who are those today who may be "excluded" or *cut off* from the community of faith? How can we make sure they have the opportunity to hear the gospel and find hope in Christ?

NOTES ──

1. Clinton E. Arnold, "Ephesians," *Zondervan Illustrated Bible Backgrounds Commentary*, vol. 3 (Grand Rapids: Zondervan, 2002), 317.

FOCAL TEXT
Ephesians 3

BACKGROUND
Ephesians 3

MAIN IDEA
In light of the mission God has given the church, the church needs God's strength and for Christ and his love to dwell in the hearts of its members.

QUESTION TO EXPLORE
What should be included in a prayer for your church?

STUDY AIM
To evaluate the extent to which I recognize the mission to which God has set the church and to identify ways for receiving spiritual strength for fulfilling it

QUICK READ
The church's mission to proclaim the gospel should prompt us to pray God will grant us the strength, love, and power to fulfill it.

LESSON FOUR
The Church's Mission, the Church's Needs

I love hearing the stories of people whose lives have been transformed by the gospel. The drug dealer who is now a deacon, the alcoholic who put down the bottle and picked up a Bible to preach, the Muslim who became a Christian missionary—I'm continually delighted by the power of the gospel to rescue and redeem. No one is beyond its reach. As the church we have the awesome responsibility of stewarding the grace of God. God could have chosen angels to proclaim his word or written the gospel across the sky. Instead, God chose us to preach Jesus to the world—even with all our weakness and frailty. Fulfilling the mission God has given the church requires spiritual strength and wisdom only God can supply. Such a mission should drive us to our knees.

EPHESIANS 3

[1] For this reason I, Paul, the prisoner of Christ Jesus for the sake of you Gentiles— [2] Surely you have heard about the administration of God's grace that was given to me for you, [3] that is, the mystery made known to me by revelation, as I have already written briefly. [4] In reading this, then, you will be able to understand my insight into the mystery of Christ, [5] which was not made known to men in other generations as it has now been revealed by the Spirit to God's holy apostles and prophets. [6] This mystery is that through the gospel the Gentiles are heirs together with Israel, members together of one body, and sharers together in the promise in Christ Jesus. [7] I became a servant of this gospel by the gift of God's grace given me through the working of his power. [8] Although I am less than the least of all God's people, this grace was given me: to preach to the Gentiles the unsearchable riches of Christ, [9] and to make plain to everyone the administration of this mystery, which for ages past was kept hidden in God, who created all things. [10] His intent was that now, through the church, the manifold wisdom of God should be made known to the rulers and authorities in the heavenly realms, [11] according to his eternal purpose which he accomplished in Christ Jesus our Lord. [12] In him and through faith in him we may approach God with freedom and

confidence. [13] I ask you, therefore, not to be discouraged because of my sufferings for you, which are your glory.

[14] For this reason I kneel before the Father, [15] from whom his whole family in heaven and on earth derives its name. [16] I pray that out of his glorious riches he may strengthen you with power through his Spirit in your inner being, [17] so that Christ may dwell in your hearts through faith. And I pray that you, being rooted and established in love, [18] may have power, together with all the saints, to grasp how wide and long and high and deep is the love of Christ, [19] and to know this love that surpasses knowledge—that you may be filled to the measure of all the fullness of God. [20] Now to him who is able to do immeasurably more than all we ask or imagine, according to his power that is at work within us, [21] to him be glory in the church and in Christ Jesus throughout all generations, for ever and ever! Amen.

Stewards of Grace (3:1–13)

In chapter 3 Paul described himself as "the prisoner of Christ Jesus for the sake of you Gentiles" (Ephesians 3:1). Paul's passion for preaching Christ to the Gentiles had directly led to his imprisonment. A Jewish mob had risen up against Paul in Jerusalem and accused him of bringing Gentiles into the temple (Acts 21:27–32). The charges were false, but it was Paul's love for the Gentiles that had incited the crowd against him. Even so, Paul did not back away from his message. He continued to proclaim the "mystery" that the prophets and priests had never fully understood. God's intentions had always been bigger than the salvation of Israel; God would be satisfied with nothing less than the salvation of the world. Paul understood that "through the gospel the Gentiles are heirs together with Israel, members together of one body, and sharers together in the promise in Christ Jesus" (Eph. 3:6). A prison cell did not have the power to shake Paul from his message.

Paul did not regard his mission as a burdensome responsibility but a God-given opportunity. For Paul, being able to preach Christ to the Gentiles was a gift of God's grace. Twice in Ephesians 3 Paul referred to the "administration" of God's grace (3:2, 9). The Greek word here translated "administration" is used to describe the work of the overseer or steward of an estate—the person who was responsible for properly running the estate in the owner's absence and who would be accountable to the owner upon his return. It was Paul's mission to administer or manage God's grace by proclaiming it to the Gentiles.

The administration of God's grace was not only Paul's responsibility. It belongs to the church as well. As the church, we steward the grace of God by proclaiming it to those who have not heard. We are participants in a cosmic mission. God's wisdom is revealed in the church to "the rulers and authorities in the heavenly realms" (Eph. 3:10). Through the church God's wisdom is revealed to the spiritual powers that affect human life. Both angels and demons bear witness to God's power and wisdom revealed in the lives of sinners redeemed and made whole. Although the cross may have seemed foolish to both earthly and spiritual powers, the victorious church is an emphatic declaration of God's eternal wisdom. It is what God had planned all along: to gather a people from every tribe and tongue whose redemption would testify to his glory.

God's eternal purposes were accomplished in Christ, and through Christ "we may approach God with freedom and confidence"(Eph. 3:12). The word Paul used for "freedom" in verse 12 was used in Greek literature to describe the kind of communication that occurs between close friends. It describes open, honest, and truthful conversation.[1] When I'm with good friends, I'm able to relax in conversation. I don't have to worry about things being taken wrong, and I don't feel guilty asking them to do me a favor. Jesus said that he no longer called us servants, but friends (John 15:15). We don't have to approach God as servants fearing their master's disapproval. We can come before God freely and confidently as we would talk to a friend. That spirit of freedom and boldness should impact how we pray for the church.

A Prayer for Power (3:14–21)

In Ephesians 3:14 Paul returned to his thought from 3:1. Knowing that the church is built together as a building for God's Spirit (Eph. 2:22) undergirds Paul's prayer for the church that begins in 3:14. Paul described his posture in prayer as *kneeling* or *bowing my knees*. Although we recognize kneeling as a typical posture for prayer, it wasn't a common position for Jewish prayer. Most Jewish men would stand to pray.[2] Kneeling, however, was a posture that communicated deep respect. We have the freedom to come before God as a friend, but we must also never forget that he is Lord.

Paul addressed his prayer to the Father, "from whom his whole family in heaven and on earth derives its name" (3:15). In the Bible, names carried deep significance, and giving a person a name was important. Naming a person or thing indicated that the namer in some sense had power or authority over the one named. Names were also important in the Greek world. Some believed that learning the name of a spirit gave the power to command that spirit.[3] Recognizing that God is the namer of "his whole family in heaven and on earth" is a recognition that God is Creator of all. All the peoples of the earth fall under God's authority, and God also has power over all other spiritual forces. Prayer must flow from a knowledge of who God is. As we pray for the church, we come before the God who is our loving Father and also the ultimate power over all creation.

Paul prayed that "out of his glorious riches he may strengthen you with power through his Spirit in your inner being" (3:16). It's important

Z.N. MORRELL: FRONTIER PREACHER

As Z.N. Morrell and his family crossed the Texas-Louisiana border in 1836, they were met by a stream of people fleeing Texas. The fleeing crowds told him that Santa Anna was victorious at the Alamo and it was only a matter of time before Santa Anna's army purged Texas of Anglo settlers. Even so, Morrell was resolute that God had called him to Texas, and he and his family pressed ahead. When word reached Morrell about Sam Houston's victory at San Jacinto, Morrell took it as confirmation of his faith.

For fifty years Morrell traveled the state of Texas. He preached, baptized, and planted churches wherever he went. He believed God had given him a promise that the Texas "wilderness would yet blossom as the rose." This faith undergirded Morrell's passion for preaching on the frontier. Although he himself lacked formal education, Morrell was instrumental in helping found Baylor University. Morrell helped build the foundation of Texas Baptist life.[4]

to note that Paul used plural pronouns throughout this section. We often claim this prayer for ourselves as individuals, but the experience of being strengthened by God's Spirit is something we experience corporately as his church. Paul prayed that we would be empowered by God's Spirit in the "inner being"—our hearts, or that part of ourselves that communicates with God and is renewed as part of the new creation. It's not a half-hearted prayer. In Ephesians 1 Paul went to great lengths to describe the magnitude of the glorious riches of God's grace (see lesson 1). Here Paul prayed that we might experience spiritual power in accordance with the magnitude of God's wealth. In the heat of summer, some cities experience rolling blackouts due to strains on the power grid. There is no such limit on spiritual power. Our power in the church flows directly from the inexhaustible resources of the Spirit.

This power is not without purpose. God strengthens us with his power "so that Christ may dwell in your hearts through faith" (3:17). Again, this is a corporate experience. God lives in the hearts of believers through the Holy Spirit, but Christ also dwells among us when we come together as the people of faith. We cannot fully experience the power and person of Jesus Christ as individuals. Faith is a team sport. It takes the church coming together as the body of Christ for us to fully realize the power of the risen Christ living in our midst.

Paul also prayed that we "may have power, together with all the saints, to grasp how wide and long and high and deep is the love of Christ, and to know this love that surpasses knowledge —that you may be filled to the measure of all the fullness of God" (3:18–19). Knowing God's love transforms us. The love that bound Jesus to the cross has no limits. *Knowing* in the Bible almost always goes beyond mere intellectual understanding. It is a knowledge built out of experience as we pursue Christ together. Somehow in the great mysteries of God, God's power enables us to know that which surpasses knowledge—the depth and the breadth of the love of Christ. It is in knowing and experiencing God's love that we are "filled to the measure of all the fullness of God" (3:19). This is something we must do together. The love of God cannot be fully comprehended in isolation. It is something we can understand only as we live life together with God's people. We begin to grasp it as we realize that no one is outside the reach of God's love; we come to know it as others give us grace for our own failures; we experience it as God's love

---

WAYS TO PRAY FOR YOUR CHURCH

- Pray that God would strengthen your church's sense of mission in your community and that God would show you how you can be a part of that mission.
- Pray for your congregation to grow in unity and in the knowledge and experience of the love of God.
- Pray that God will give your church a task that requires God's strength to accomplish.
- Pray that your church will be a good steward of the gospel. Ask that God would open your eyes to those in your community who need to hear the good news.

---

flowing through us to those he also loves. It takes a church to know the fullness of God's love.

Paul concluded his prayer with a stirring doxology: "Now to him who is able to do immeasurably more than all we ask or imagine, according to his power that is at work within us, to him be glory in the church and in Christ Jesus throughout all generations, for ever and ever! Amen" (3:20–21). It is impossible to ask God for too much. God's power and generosity toward his church far surpass what we could ask or even imagine. God has entrusted his church with the God-sized task of proclaiming the grace of God throughout all generations. It is our joyous responsibility to glorify God.

Implications and Actions

As the church, our mission is to glorify God by proclaiming and living the gospel. It is a task that requires spiritual strength only God can supply. We begin to access that power through our own relationship with God. Yet we cannot fully pursue Christ on our own. There are depths in God that we can access only in relationship with one another. Although we all have roles to play, the task of proclaiming the gospel was given to the church. We can only accomplish this task together.

Gospel proclamation must always be undergirded by prayer. Prayer unites us with God and with one another. When we pray for the church, we come confidently before our God, who is both Father and Creator of all. We pray for more power and knowledge of God. We pray for a deeper understanding of God's love that overflows into a love for God's people, and we pray with the confidence that we cannot ask for more than God can give. Fulfilling God's mission can be accomplished only by God's power and love demonstrated in the hearts of God's people.

QUESTIONS

1. What is your church's mission? How do you participate in that mission?

2. Do you think it is true that there are some truths about God we can understand and experience only as a part of the Christian community? Why?

3. How have you experienced the power and grace of God as revealed by the church?

4. What connection does our understanding of God's love have with spiritual strength?

5. What difference does it make to your prayers for your church to know that our God can do "immeasurably more than all we ask or imagine" (Eph. 3:20)?

NOTES

1. Clinton E. Arnold, "Ephesians," in *Zondervan Illustrated Bible Backgrounds Commentary*, vol. 3 (Grand Rapids: Zondervan, 2002), 321; see "Parrhesia" in *Theological Dictionary of The New Testament*, abridged edition (William B. Eerdmans).

2. Andrew T. Lincoln, *Ephesians*, Word Biblical Commentary (Nashville: Thomas Nelson, 1990), 201.

3. Arnold, 311.

4. Harry Leon McBeth, *Texas Baptists: A Sesquicentennial History* (Dallas, Texas: BaptistWay Press, 1998), 15–18.

FOCAL TEXT
Ephesians 4:1–16

BACKGROUND
Ephesians 4:1–16

MAIN IDEA
The church is to live in a
manner worthy of its calling
as the body of Christ.

QUESTION TO EXPLORE
What qualities of Christ does
your church demonstrate?

STUDY AIM
To identify qualities and
actions the church is to
demonstrate as Christ's body

QUICK READ
God calls Christian people to
be united in fellowship and
service, striving to model their
experience after Christ himself.

LESSON FIVE
The Church Fulfilling Its Calling

I have a letter that my grandmother wrote to her mother on July 31, 1899. Grandmother had traveled in a horse-drawn wagon from Northeast Georgia through the mountains to visit relatives in North Carolina. Among the many treasures in the letter were her comments about church: "Went to meeting yesterday. Preacher Stoner preached. There was a big crowd there, I expect there was 25 or 30, and such singing has never been heard. Grandpa said it was the best he ever saw." That was church in 1899 from the viewpoint of a seventeen-year-old, but can you imagine what church was like thirty years after Jesus' death?

In Ephesus, Christians from Jewish and non-Jewish backgrounds probably gathered in a home, seeking to find their way in this new experience with God and with one another. They were excited to have a letter from Paul, the great apostle. They read the doctrinal and theological sections of Ephesians (chapters 1–3), and then they turned to the more practical section. The first words of Ephesians 4 were for them to live a life worthy of their calling as followers of Jesus Christ. Paul said living in this way was urgent. They would read more about unity, gifts, spiritual maturity, morality, family life, and other subjects, but this was Paul's beginning point in making the gospel message practical: "live a life worthy of the calling you have received" (Ephesians 4:1).[1]

Ephesians 4:1–16

[1] As a prisoner for the Lord, then, I urge you to live a life worthy of the calling you have received. [2] Be completely humble and gentle; be patient, bearing with one another in love. [3] Make every effort to keep the unity of the Spirit through the bond of peace. [4] There is one body and one Spirit— just as you were called to one hope when you were called— [5] one Lord, one faith, one baptism; [6] one God and Father of all, who is over all and through all and in all. [7] But to each one of us grace has been given as Christ apportioned it. [8] This is why it says: "When he ascended on high, he led captives in his train and gave gifts to men." [9] (What does "he ascended" mean except that he also descended to the lower, earthly regions? [10] He who descended is the very one who ascended higher than all the heavens, in order to fill the whole

universe.) [11] It was he who gave some to be apostles, some to be prophets, some to be evangelists, and some to be pastors and teachers, [12] to prepare God's people for works of service, so that the body of Christ may be built up [13] until we all reach unity in the faith and in the knowledge of the Son of God and become mature, attaining to the whole measure of the fullness of Christ. [14] Then we will no longer be infants, tossed back and forth by the waves, and blown here and there by every wind of teaching and by the cunning and craftiness of men in their deceitful scheming. [15] Instead, speaking the truth in love, we will in all things grow up into him who is the Head, that is, Christ. [16] From him the whole body, joined and held together by every supporting ligament, grows and builds itself up in love, as each part does its work.

The Church United (4:1–6)

Our calling as Christians begins with a call to salvation through Jesus Christ, which entails a new beginning or a new birth, a fresh start at life. Living worthy of that experience and calling is important. To do so, Paul mentioned Christian virtues each believer should practice: humility, gentleness, patience, and "bearing with one another in love" (Eph. 4:2). Humility means being down to earth, not on an ego trip. Gentleness is a spirit and conduct that is disciplined but not abrasive, handling people and relationships with kindness. Patience implies a calm and long commitment in dealing with yourself and others. Sometime we humans are hard to put up with, but we still are called to bear "with one another in love." We are to see people with eyes of love. These qualities are seen in Jesus, and they need to be qualities that describe our churches and individual lives.

God did not save us in order for us to fly solo through the universe but to fly together. Being born again means that we enter into a family with brothers and sisters in Christ. Thus, God is the source of our unity. The fact that we are linked together is established by God; the issue is how do we maintain and reveal that unity. The previous individual virtues have implications for how we maintain that unity. They help us achieve the blessing of unity. Sometimes the practice of unity is difficult to achieve or maintain; however, its difficulty is no excuse. God expects our move from individual conversion to living as a good family member to go well. We should do all we can do to make sure that happens (see Romans 12:18; 1 Peter 3:11).

I passed a church and noted its sign, "The Harmony Baptist Church." *A good name*, I thought. A few miles later, I passed another church, "The New Harmony Baptist Church." Did something happen to the harmony? Unity is not a small thing to God, and many of our disruptions of fellowship reflect the absence of the four qualities mentioned in verse 2—humility, gentleness, patience, and forbearance. Paul wrote an instructive parallel to this Scripture in Philippians 2:1–11.

Notice the *ones* in verses 4–6: "one body," "one Spirit," "one hope," "one Lord," "one faith," "one baptism," "one God and Father." Consider what each means to our unity. Paul mentioned God as our Father as the last unifier; perhaps that's another reminder that the children do not choose the people with whom they will be united. The common word, however, is "one." Paul was not talking of independence but interdependence. Although the church may be made up of diverse people, we need to be good practitioners of unity. Does the world think of us because of our love and oneness? See John 13:34–35 to see what Jesus said about that.

The Church Using Gifts (4:7–13)

We may come into the church one-at-a-time, but we immediately are part of a group, the body of Christ. We also become part of God's plan for fulfilling God's mission in the world: "To each one of us grace has been given as Christ apportioned it" (Eph. 4:7). Grace is often defined as God's unmerited love or favor, a love we have not deserved or earned. In this passage, grace refers to the gifts of God. Everyone is gifted, and none of us have earned it. God gave it, and so do not brag about or whine over your gift, or think less of yourself because you do not have someone else's gift. As Paul also wrote, "to each one the manifestation of the Spirit is given for the common good" (1 Corinthians 12:7). All God's people are gifted people and, gratefully, not all in the same way. Unity and diversity go together.

The gifts mentioned in verse 11 deal with the *management and leadership team* of the church. Apostles, prophets, evangelists, and pastors-teachers represent something of the historical development of early church leaders. Jesus called the Twelve to follow him in a special way. After the resurrection, they were known as apostles, for they physically had been with Jesus. Today we could think of apostles in terms of missionaries. Prophets were people who boldly spoke God's word. Prophecy was not always predictive. Some think these first two categories passed away with the New Testament era, but many today still speak prophetically about the needs of the world from a Christian perspective. Evangelists were those with a special ability to reach non-Christian people. Paul charged Timothy to "do the work of an evangelist" (2 Timothy 4:5). The last mentioned in the list, pastor-teacher, is probably one office.

The pastor-teacher has some specific roles: (1) prepare God's people to minister; (2) build up the church in unity around Jesus Christ; and (3) help the church mature spiritually. "Pastor" grows out of the word for shepherd. Jesus is identified as The Good Shepherd (John 10:11; 1 Peter 5:1–4). This pastoral role today is often summarized as one who preaches, teaches, cares, and leads. Those words reflect biblical language, but we must not misunderstand the first role: prepare God's people for

GIFTS, CREATIVE AND SPIRITUAL

Gifts are sometimes thought of as talents or abilities that we have from birth; thus, someone is a gifted singer, teacher, or athlete. We should be good stewards in developing and using these creative gifts; however, I know that no amount of work can take someone like me and transform him or her into a gifted singer. These gifts, valuable as they are, were not the focus of Paul's instruction on gifts.

Spiritual gifts are endowments from God that come to believers and are not based on creation but on a relationship to Christ. These gifts are designed to help you fulfill God's purpose for the church and your purpose in life. In addition to Ephesians 4:7–13, see Romans 12:6–8; 1 Corinthians 12:8–11, 27–30; and 1 Peter 4:10–11 for information on spiritual gifts. These Scriptures do not list everything God does to gift the church; however, seek to see which of these fits who you are in Christ. Everyone is gifted by God. Use your gifts well.

ministry. We sometimes attach the word *minister* to the professionals, thinking we have hired a pastor or staff to minister. They will minister, but you can never hire someone to fulfill your personal role to minister to people. The pastor is to equip you, to help you to minister and serve, to use your gifts more effectively.

In Mark 10:45, Jesus said that he came into the world not to be ministered unto but to minister. Thus, it is no surprise that when God saves people to become the church and gifts people to lead the church, then God also expects all of them to have the servant mentality that Jesus had. When we do, we indeed live a life worthy of our calling. Today, churches do not struggle for lack of gifts, but rather churches struggle when we do not use our gifts in ways that honor God and meet the needs of others.

In Ephesians 4:8–9, Paul referred to Christ and how he was the fulfillment of Psalm 68:18. That often happens in the writing of Paul. When he mentions Christ, he is moved to say a word of praise or identify something of the gospel. Here Paul referred to both the incarnation (God in human flesh) of Jesus and also to Jesus' resurrection and ascension into heaven. In so doing, as Paul interpreted the psalm, people were freed to follow Christ and gifted to serve him. That still happens. That's what church is about.

The Church Grows Up (4:14–16)

When our children were growing up, they occasionally had sharp words for each other. One line was, "You are so immature." Although they often were right, their attitudes were not. Can you imagine an eight-year-old telling her fourteen-year-old sister, "You are so immature"? Gratefully, they all matured enough to outgrow that tendency to speak harshly and critically to each other, generally speaking. Christians can speak the truth in love to one another, and that can become part of the growing process for all. When love is not our motivator, we sow the seeds of discord.

What about *your* church? What about *your* maturity? Most of us can conjecture how good we are when we compare ourselves to others, but Paul took that out of the mix. Our standard of comparison and standard of maturity is Christ. When we recognize this standard, we know that we have unfinished business in maturity.

TALK THE WALK

The Greek word for "live a life" in Ephesians 4:1 is *peripatesai,* which means *to walk around.* It refers to a lifestyle or constant demeanor. We sometimes speak of *walking the talk*, but consider how you can *talk the walk*. Talk the church up, not down.

- Use your words to reflect well on Christ
- Use your words to build unity
- Use your words to help people understand their giftedness
- Use your words to encourage church leaders
- Use your words to inspire maturity in Christ
- Use your words to help the church operate effectively and smoothly

Even so, the Bible also teaches us that God "knows how we are formed" (Psalm 103:14). If God wants something done, God has no perfect people to do it. So, serve God as best you can, seek to be as mature as you can, but know that the standard is high and you never reach it. On the other hand, striving for the higher standard allows you to go higher than you ever dreamed possible (Eph. 3:20). See Paul's testimony about this in Philippians 3:12–16.

Immature Christians are adults who are still spiritual infants. Using a different image, Paul said they were like boats in a storm, being tossed to and fro. The problem was they were not growing and were deficient "in the faith and knowledge of the Son of God" (Eph. 4:13). They were easily swayed by false teachers and teachings. Paul also saw the better side of the Ephesians. He believed they would "grow up into him who is the Head, that is, Christ" (4:15).

Notice in verse 16 the concluding picture of the church. The body responds to the leadership of the head; the church grows because of Christ. What does that look like? Paul wrote that it was a body where the parts were working correctly, where love was causing growth to happen, and where every part of the body did what his or her part should do. That's a lofty vision, but that vision is still possible for any church.

Meaning for Today

The church is instructed to demonstrate a lifestyle that is worthy of its calling as the body of Christ. If the church is to mirror Christ, then the church helps people find peace with God and live peacefully with each other. God gifts his people to continue the work of Christ on earth. Church leaders and members are expected to follow the example of Christ, the ultimate model of servanthood.

The church's founder and head "grew in wisdom and stature and in favor with God and men" (Luke 2:52). Growth and maturity are also expected of all Christians. When the church functions as God envisions, it is a thriving body motivated by and revealing the love of God.

Unity is a focal point in this lesson's Scripture as well as in Ephesians 2:11–22 and 3:14–21. Jesus prayed for unity among his followers (John 17). A famous basketball player was asked the secret of his team's success. The interviewer noted that individually their talents were often not as good as other teams' players. The player said, "Yes, you are right, but we are good enough. The key is that we realize we have only one ball to play with." Playing together encourages your teammates, maximizes your gifts, and helps your team—church—fulfill its purpose.

QUESTIONS

1. What qualities of Christ do your class and your church need to exhibit more?

2. Paul had a sense of urgency about "living a life worthy." Would you describe your understanding of this truth as something urgent or just something nice?

3. Who among your Bible class or friends does the best job of building up the unity of the church? If these folks answered this question, would they think of you? Why or why not?

4. Since maturity is a goal, what area of your life can you focus on in the next seven days to become more what God wants you to be?

5. What affect does *oneness* have on your church's or class's ability to attract new members?

6. How well are you using the gifts and opportunities you have been given?

NOTES

1. Unless otherwise indicated, all Scripture quotations in lessons 1–13 are from the New International Version (1984 edition).

FOCAL TEXT
Ephesians 4:17—5:20

BACKGROUND
Ephesians 4:17—5:20

MAIN IDEA

Members of Christ's body
are to change their way of
living to the way of Christ.

QUESTION TO EXPLORE

To what extent do your
daily behaviors reflect
the way of Christ?

STUDY AIM

To describe the teachings
about Christian living in
this passage and to decide to
implement the one that is most
difficult for me to practice

QUICK READ

When we live a "life worthy of
our calling" (4:1), our lifestyle
will reflect God's standards,
not only in unity in the church
but also Christ-honoring
behavior in the world.

LESSON SIX
Live the New Way of Christ

One of my heroes is a brilliant man of deep faith. He is so disciplined in his time and so devout in his faith. One day he said to me, "I am appalled at what I am no longer appalled at." That comment was stunning. He was not satisfied with who he was becoming. Perhaps you can identify with him. As you study the principles in this lesson, consider which is the most difficult for you to follow. Among those good and bad examples of behavior in this lesson, identify at least one that you will make a deliberate effort to bring into harmony with God's will and purpose.

EPHESIANS 4:17–32

[17] So I tell you this, and insist on it in the Lord, that you must no longer live as the Gentiles do, in the futility of their thinking. [18] They are darkened in their understanding and separated from the life of God because of the ignorance that is in them due to the hardening of their hearts. [19] Having lost all sensitivity, they have given themselves over to sensuality so as to indulge in every kind of impurity, with a continual lust for more. [20] You, however, did not come to know Christ that way. [21] Surely you heard of him and were taught in him in accordance with the truth that is in Jesus. [22] You were taught, with regard to your former way of life, to put off your old self, which is being corrupted by its deceitful desires; [23] to be made new in the attitude of your minds; [24] and to put on the new self, created to be like God in true righteousness and holiness. [25] Therefore each of you must put off falsehood and speak truthfully to his neighbor, for we are all members of one body. [26] "In your anger do not sin": Do not let the sun go down while you are still angry, [27] and do not give the devil a foothold. [28] He who has been stealing must steal no longer, but must work, doing something useful with his own hands, that he may have something to share with those in need. [29] Do not let any unwholesome talk come out of your mouths, but only what is helpful for building others up according to their needs, that it may benefit those who listen. [30] And do not grieve the Holy Spirit of God, with whom you were sealed for the day of redemption. [31] Get rid of all bitterness, rage and anger, brawling and slander, along with every form of

malice. [32] Be kind and compassionate to one another, forgiving each other, just as in Christ God forgave you.

EPHESIANS 5:1–20

[1] Be imitators of God, therefore, as dearly loved children [2] and live a life of love, just as Christ loved us and gave himself up for us as a fragrant offering and sacrifice to God. [3] But among you there must not be even a hint of sexual immorality, or of any kind of impurity, or of greed, because these are improper for God's holy people. [4] Nor should there be obscenity, foolish talk or coarse joking, which are out of place, but rather thanksgiving. [5] For of this you can be sure: No immoral, impure or greedy person—such a man is an idolater—has any inheritance in the kingdom of Christ and of God. [6] Let no one deceive you with empty words, for because of such things God's wrath comes on those who are disobedient. [7] Therefore do not be partners with them. [8] For you were once darkness, but now you are light in the Lord. Live as children of light [9] (for the fruit of the light consists in all goodness, righteousness and truth) [10] and find out what pleases the Lord. [11] Have nothing to do with the fruitless deeds of darkness, but rather expose them. [12] For it is shameful even to mention what the disobedient do in secret. [13] But everything exposed by the light becomes visible, [14] for it is light that makes everything visible. This is why it is said: "Wake up, O sleeper, rise from the dead, and Christ will shine on you." [15] Be very careful, then, how you live—not as unwise but as wise, [16] making the most of every opportunity, because the days are evil. [17] Therefore do not be foolish, but understand what the Lord's will is. [18] Do not get drunk on wine, which leads to debauchery. Instead, be filled with the Spirit. [19] Speak to one another with psalms, hymns and spiritual songs. Sing and make music in your heart to the Lord, [20] always giving thanks to God the Father for everything, in the name of our Lord Jesus Christ.

Off with the Old, On with the New (4:17–24)

As the Ephesians worked through the implications of living a life worthy of their calling, Paul stressed unity within a maturing body of believers in the church. Paul then turned his attention to how their lives should be different from the pagan culture around them. Some did not have the ethical background of Judaism, and so Paul went back to the basics. He called for them to make a clean break from their pre-Christian background. Some of what he wrote seems so elementary, but if he were writing in the light of our culture today, would his ethical teaching reflect a society that was in touch with the high ideals of Christianity or a world gone astray? Are our lives distinctly different because of Christ?

Notice Paul's description of people in the first century. Their approach to life revealed minds that were clueless about God, hearts hardened to God's will, and behavior that seemed to reveal no conscience or sensitivity to the better things of life. They indulged "in every kind of impurity, with a continual lust for more." Paul was not accusing the Ephesian church with being so depraved, but he did know that their temptations were tough and their lapses in behavior did not honor Christ.

Even though the members of the Ephesian church might have been relatively new to the Christian faith, they knew Jesus Christ, had learned the ways of Christ, and had grown as believers. Since they were not in the first days of their Christian experience, Paul reaffirmed his earlier call (Ephesians 4:14–16) for them to grow up and show maturity not only in understanding Christ, but also in how they lived the Christian life in the world. Worship in the church is vital but so is living the faith in the world.

Paul used a metaphor of clothing to make his point, although Paul certainly did not believe the changes demanded by the Christian life were to be only cosmetic. Take the old off and put on the new. Get rid of your old self and behaviors, and put on the new. Paul knew that it was an *inside-out* change: "to be made new in the attitude of your minds and to put on the new self" (Eph. 4:23–24). The pattern for this transformation is one that seeks to mirror God in both righteousness and holiness. This teaching is found often in Scripture, with Romans 12:1–3 being worthy of a parallel study.

JAMES'S VIEW OF THE WAY WE TALK

The Book of James teaches us to "be quick to listen, slow to speak and slow to become angry" (James 1:19). James also notes that we should "keep a tight rein" on our tongues (James 1:26). In a longer section on this subject, James 3:1–12, James wrote that "no man can tame the tongue" (James 3:8). He does not imply that we hopelessly say the wrong things and that it is inevitable that we keep at least one foot in our mouth.

On our own, without God's strength, much of our efforts are in vain, but Christians do not do life in their own strength. We understand that God is involved in our lives. We know that with God's help, we can certainly do better in accentuating the positive use of language and keeping a "tight rein" on our tongues. Don't forget: God never asks us to do anything he will not help us achieve.

Getting Specific About the Christian Options to Sin (4:25–32)

When I was a young minister, my father was always supportive, and rarely would he say anything negative about my preaching or teaching. He had plenty of opportunities, I am sure, but that was just not his way. On one occasion, however, we were discussing the sermon, and I probed him a little deeper. Finally, he said, "Well, it was a really good sermon, but it suffered a little from a lack of specificity." I got the point. Paul was not writing a scholarly paper. Rather he probably was dealing with specific issues that kept the Ephesian church from having an impact in the world that it should.

Paul knew the Ephesian people. "The saints in Ephesus" (Eph. 1:1) were not living like saints in the world. Several members must have not been telling the truth. You may have heard this twisting of a Bible verse: "A lie is an ever present help in time of need." Maybe so, but that ought not to be true among Christians. Notice the imperatives: no more lying, no unwholesome talk, no slander (4:25, 29, 31). Paul had already written for them to "speak the truth in love" (4:15); now he built on that comment. Speak truthfully, speak in ways that build people up and benefit those who listen, and be ready to speak words of kindness and forgiveness (4:32).

Anger is a human emotion that can be controlled (4:26). As Christians, we are to control our speech and actions in ways that reflect well on Christ's purpose. Sometimes it is a sin not to be angry, for some conditions in our world demand more than just a wrinkled eyebrow or a groan. Even then, however, we are to recognize that exceptional circumstances do not justify a constant spirit of anger and malice. Most of us would be better if we practiced the *biblical sunset rule* on anger.

Paul taught a work ethic that is also reflected in other portions of Scripture. Evidently, some converts had made a living by stealing. Instead of stealing, Paul wrote that persons should work, doing something useful with their hands. Notice part of the motive: so that you "may have something to share with those in need" (4:28). His ethic was that rather than taking from those who have, you are to share with those who have not. Christian hands were not made for stealing but for working and sharing.

"Do not grieve the Holy Spirit of God" is a realization that all sin is ultimately a slap in the face of God (4:30). Lying, stealing, and uncontrolled anger are sins against people, but they also reflect an abuse of God. In the Old Testament, Potiphar's wife was tempting Joseph to have sex with her. Joseph refused, saying, "How then could I do such a wicked thing and sin against God?" (Genesis 39:9). All sin is ultimately a sin against God. God is grieved by our sin.

Forgiveness is important in the Christian faith. God's forgiveness is part of the process when we become believers in Jesus Christ. God forgives us for our sin and through Christ makes it possible for us to have a fresh start on life. God then expects forgiven people to be forgiving people (see The Lord's Prayer, Matthew 6:9–15). Perhaps offering forgiveness is the kindest thing we can do for other people. When we forgive, we do not hold their past against them but rather give them a fresh start in relationship with ourselves and with others. Kind, compassionate, and forgiving—that's the way God is, and that is what God expects from us in speech and in behavior.

Ephesians 4 closes with a summary of actions and attitudes to avoid, as well as a positive word about kindness, compassion, and forgiveness. Many of us have been in Sunday School all of our lives and somewhere along the way we began to memorize Bible verses. I cannot remember when I learned it, but I have known basically all of my life "Be ye kind one to another" (Eph. 4:32, KJV). Some of the most difficult verses to practice faithfully are the simplest.

Live as Imitators of God (5:1–7)

Paul wrote about moral principles and specific actions that should characterize our behavior; however, he added a new motivation: "Be imitators of God, therefore, as dearly loved children, and live a life of love" (Eph. 5:1). Paul wrote in Ephesians 4:24 that we have been "created to be like God in true righteousness and holiness." Here Paul called the church "God's holy people" (5:3). The root meaning of "holy" is *different*. The Spirit of God is holy because God's Spirit is different from any other spirit. The temple was called holy for it was different from any other building. The Bible is holy for it is different from any other book. Likewise, we should be holy, different because God is empowering us to change in ways that help us become more like him. The result is that we become more able to live a life that honors God, enriches others, and satisfies our own selves. We learn and grow into living "a life of love" (5:2) because God in Christ is our ultimate pattern for life.

Paul continued to call the Ephesians to be different from the world around them. He called for sexual purity. Sexual immorality was rampant in Ephesus, with hundreds of prostitutes working through the Temple of Diana. Paul added sexual immorality, obscenity, dirty talk, greed, and deceptive speech to the list of things that are inappropriate and sinful for Christians. Not only should we not do these things, but also we should not "be partners with" those who do such things (5:7). That lifestyle is not what the Christian life is about. As the Ephesians were learning more about Christ and the kingdom of God, they were also understanding that God forbids such behavior from his children and will bring judgment on those who practice it.

Live as Children of Light (5:8–14)

Paul continued to contrast the old way of life for the Ephesians with the life they now had in Christ. He used common religious symbolism of light and darkness. Although Christians once were darkness, they now were light. Thus, they should "live as children of light" (5:8). Jesus himself referred to his disciples as "the light of the world" (Matt. 5:14). He taught them that their light should be seen in the world, and that outsiders would then see the goodness that God can do in a person's life (Matt. 5:15). Paul was clear that a life in the light produces goodness, righteousness, and truth. In so doing, he also taught that we have a responsibility to expose the darkness to the light and seek to make the world around us more pleasing to the Lord.

Live Wisely (5:15–20)

Many teachers have said to their classes, *Pay attention*. Paul the teacher said something similar. He wrote, "Be very careful, then, how you live— not as unwise, but as wise" (Eph. 5:15). He mentioned another large motivator: "understand what the Lord's will is" (5:17). Understanding is not the same as doing, but Paul's purpose was for them to do the Lord's will. Another specific issue is mentioned, drunkenness. We sometimes speak of alcohol abuse, but drunkenness is not really about abusing alcohol. Rather, it involves abusing others and ourselves, thus reflecting poorly on Christ and his people. Problem drinking is still a significant issue in our world and among Christians.

On the positive side, Paul wrote, "be filled with the Spirit" (5:18). Sometimes people are fearful of such an instruction, afraid that they are going to do something strange or erratic. Alcohol can do that, but God does not. Being filled with the Spirit will give you more power, love, and self control than you ever imagined (2 Timothy 1:7). Let God fill your life, for God is always working for his good pleasure and that is always good for us (Philippians 2:13).

Paul's concluding word in this section is a word of thanksgiving (Eph. 5:20). Thanksgiving is always in season. Regardless of our circumstances, we all have been blessed by God and others in ways that we only partially understand. When we look for other positive uses of speech, don't forget to be thankful. That specific action can change your life as well as the lives of others.

Putting Faith into Practice

Practice what you preach is clear, Bible-based advice. What we profess is what we should practice consistently. Paul wrote often about the practical dimensions for being faithful and avoiding sin. How are we to view these? Obviously, we do not want to water down the demands of the Christian life, but Christianity is not boiled down to those who keep the rules the best.

Most games have rules, boundaries, and goals. Somewhere along the way we figure out what the game is about, and we learn that some things are fair and some are foul. Some actions lead to penalties, and some lead to victory. In life, we need to recognize that some things are not consistent with the way of Christ. We especially need to do the good things that God expects.

Good behavior is the *result* of our relationship to God; it does not create that relationship. We may not always get everything right, but we should practice what we preach, making sure that both what we preach and what we practice are consistent with God's will. When we do, we will enjoy life more as well as make life more enjoyable for others. We also would do well to leave the score-keeping to God.

QUESTIONS

1. What remnants of a non-Christian way of life are present in your life?

2. When is the last time you got really angry? How does this lesson's Scripture relate to the way you handled yourself in that experience?

3. What are the characteristics of wholesome speech that Paul mentioned?

4. How can you make the most of your opportunities to affect someone who is outside the fellowship of your church?

5. What positive changes have you seen in your life since you became a Christian?

6. Within your class, is there someone who needs a kind word or action from you?

FOCAL TEXT
Ephesians 5:21—6:9

BACKGROUND
Ephesians 5:21—6:9

MAIN IDEA

All relationships in the Christian household are to be ordered by reverence for Christ.

QUESTION TO EXPLORE

How does Christian faith affect relationships at home and at work—or does it?

STUDY AIM

To describe differences that would result if I ordered my home and work relationships by reverence for Christ

QUICK READ

The Bible offers help to us in our most basic human relationships as we live out our faith at home and at work.

LESSON SEVEN

Life in a Christian Household

New Christians in the first century may have wondered, *What should life be like within our families?* This section of the practical half of Ephesians has been called a *household code* that describes relationships within first-century homes. We see similar teachings in Colossians 3:18—4:1; Titus 2:1–10; and 1 Peter 2:18—3:7. Paul's readers already knew how these relationships functioned in their world. Some of Paul's teaching reflected their understanding, but when they read his words, they could see how he challenged their culture in powerful ways.

This comment should be no surprise: *interpreters differ greatly on what the focal text means.* Some interpreters envision a hierarchy of roles, with the husband and father being at the top of the hierarchy. Wives, children and slaves were to line up behind the male authoritarian figure and submit to his leadership. Others interpret differently, with the view that wives share in the leadership of the home. In this view, the guiding principle of Ephesians 5:21 affects all the relationships within this Scripture passage. Variations, not consensus, dominate interpretations of this passage.

EPHESIANS 5:21–33

21 Submit to one another out of reverence for Christ.

22 Wives, submit to your husbands as to the Lord. **23** For the husband is the head of the wife as Christ is the head of the church, his body, of which he is the Savior. **24** Now as the church submits to Christ, so also wives should submit to their husbands in everything. **25** Husbands, love your wives, just as Christ loved the church and gave himself up for her **26** to make her holy, cleansing her by the washing with water through the word, **27** and to present her to himself as a radiant church, without stain or wrinkle or any other blemish, but holy and blameless. **28** In this same way, husbands ought to love their wives as their own bodies. He who loves his wife loves himself. **29** After all, no one ever hated his own body, but he feeds and cares for it, just as Christ does the church— **30** for we are members of his body. **31** "For this reason a man will leave his father and mother and be united to his wife, and the two will become one flesh." **32** This is a profound mystery—but I am talking about Christ and the church. [33] However, each one of you also must love his wife as he loves himself, and the wife must respect her husband.

EPHESIANS 6:1–9

[1] Children, obey your parents in the Lord, for this is right. [2] "Honor your father and mother"—which is the first commandment with a promise— [3] "that it may go well with you and that you may enjoy long life on the earth." [4] Fathers, do not exasperate your children; instead, bring them up in the training and instruction of the Lord.

[5] Slaves, obey your earthly masters with respect and fear, and with sincerity of heart, just as you would obey Christ. [6] Obey them not only to win their favor when their eye is on you, but like slaves of Christ, doing the will of God from your heart. [7] Serve wholeheartedly, as if you were serving the Lord, not men, [8] because you know that the Lord will reward everyone for whatever good he does, whether he is slave or free. [9] And masters, treat your slaves in the same way. Do not threaten them, since you know that he who is both their Master and yours is in heaven, and there is no favoritism with him.

The Guiding Principle (5:21)

Keep in mind that our focal text begins with the teaching of mutual submission out of reverence for Christ. In Ephesians 5:18, Paul wrote, "be filled with the Spirit." Various principles grow out of that command, including mutual submission in Ephesians 5:21. Mutual submission impacts all relationships in the home, including husband/wife, parents/children, and master/slave relationships. Don't forget that principle. This section of Scripture concludes with declaring that God is not a God who shows partiality (Eph. 6:9). Earlier, in Galatians 3:28, Paul wrote "There is neither Jew nor Greek, slave nor free, male nor female, for you are all one in Christ."

Husbands and Wives (5:22–33)

In writing about marriage, Paul referred to the relationship of Christ and the church to teach us about relationships between wives and husbands. Christ is the head and Savior of the church. Christ also loved the church and died for it. Christ wanted to purify the church as holy and blameless. Christ provides sustenance to the church, feeding and caring for his people. Paul also wrote that the familiar teaching about a man leaving his mother and father and being joined to his wife is more deeply about the relationship of Christ with the church—Christ gave up heaven to come to earth, to create and be joined to the church.

Paul's first word was to wives, but his biggest challenge was to husbands. The assumption was that both husbands and wives were already submitted to the Lord and united in their faith. Both the husband and the wife were to submit to each other (Eph. 5:21), but Paul began with wives: "Wives, submit yourselves to your husbands . . ." (5:22). Actually, for wives to submit themselves to their husbands was no challenge to most of the first-century world, for that was the norm.

Headship involves leadership, and Paul wrote that wives should acknowledge that. The teaching appears to reflect the incarnate Son, Jesus Christ, being submissive to the will of the Father. The analogy between husbands and Christ is not without limits. Christ was the Savior of the church, but the husband can never be the savior of the wife. The wife's submissiveness to her husband's leadership is a voluntary one that is not coerced by the husband but entered into willingly by the wife. Again, the assumption is that both spouses are Christians.

Paul then turned to the husband, writing, "love your wives." The Greek word for "love" used here is *agape. Agape* love is a divine, sacrificial kind of love. Such love is an *I'm willing to die for you* kind of love. If a husband was willing to die for his wife, that surely would have enhanced her willingness to submit to the husband's leadership. If the husband was truly interested in helping his wife to be "radiant," "holy," and "blameless" (5:27), then the leadership option is less threatening. Paul did not spell out the implications for a husband to be submissive to his wife, but that guiding principle is best lived out by a husband loving his wife in the same manner as Christ loves us all.

Mutual submission is still the principle. Questions like these linger: *Is the emphasis on the wife submitting to the husband's headship a word from God in all situations and times, or did it have special relevance to the first century? Would this word be later superseded under the leadership of the Holy Spirit (John 16:12–13)? What about relationships where the man abuses or leaves his spouse?* The *what ifs* abound.

My understanding of the husband/wife leadership role is similar to how one interprets the slave/master issue in this same passage. Paul enhanced the status of wives and slaves. He also expanded the responsibility of husband and slave master, without condemning male leadership or slavery. As the full body of New Testament teaching grew and through the work of the Holy Spirit, the sin of slavery has been condemned, and authoritarian leadership in the home has been replaced by joint leadership, marked by mutual submission. What Paul wrote is an authentic word of God for the first-century world, but some of its application is different in the twenty-first century.

The concluding verse of this section (Eph. 5:33) is a powerful summary in which the husband is commanded to love his wife. What kind of society was evident in the first century that a husband had to be

FIRST-CENTURY BACKGROUND

In the Greek and Roman world, women sometimes had only three options: marriage, slavery, or prostitution. In Judaism, the Ten Commandments prohibited coveting one's neighbor's house, wife, servants, oxen, donkeys or "anything" that belonged to one's neighbor (Exodus 20:17). Wives were part of the *things* that people had. Then came the impact of Christian faith on a non-Christian world. Certainly it came slowly, for God was not starting a social revolution that would flame brightly and then fade out. Rather God was changing people and the culture of society, taking steps that would eventually enhance the status of women, broaden the family experience of men, and abolish slavery.

Consider this key question to answer when considering this passage and other issues that relate to women: *Are women creatures of relationships or persons with relationships? That is, is a woman simply someone's daughter or wife, or is there an identity that is wrapped up in personhood and possibility, that reflects well the creative principle of Genesis 1:27, "male and female created he them," both made in the image of God?*

commanded twice in this passage to love his wife? Again, the Greek word for love used here is *agape*, which is not a word about feeling but a word about acting in the best interest of the other party. Husbands were "to love their wives as their own bodies" (4:28). The husband who thinks of his wife in this fashion will follow the model of Christ who loved the church, the body of Christ. Wives are also to "respect" their husbands. A wife can change the atmosphere of the home by her appreciation and respect for the one she has chosen to be her husband (see 1 Peter 3:1).

Children and Parents (6:1–4)

In most cultures, children are taught to obey their parents. Paul added another dimension to that teaching: "in the Lord." Both parents are assumed to be "in the Lord." If the parents are united in the body of Christ, so too is the child. These assumptions are the ground for obedience. Children are to obey because it is the right thing to do. The family circle is not just a physical relationship, but it is also spiritual. In extreme circumstances, the child may be mature enough to say, *No, this is not right, for it is not in the Lord*; however, the norm is that we reverence Christ and recognize the role of parent and child.

"Honor your father and mother" is a command "with a promise" (Eph. 6:2–3). A meaningful understanding of this command is to live your life in such as way as to bring honor to your father and mother. In that understanding, the focus is not on whether the parent is honorable or on whether the parent is living or dead. We have the lifelong responsibility to live in such a way that it brings honor to our parents, to reflect well on them, regardless of the circumstances of the parents' lives. In the context of Ephesians, the promise is that you will be a better human being for doing so.

We have been taught that "the hand that rocks the cradle rules the world." Paul brought the focus on the role of the father, from the cradle on. Early Jewish Christians had a better understanding of being a father than their non-Jewish counterparts. Even so, all in that day were affected by a tendency toward a male authoritarian role and toward turning over the guidance of the child to the mother. Paul instructed fathers not to frustrate and cause children to be unnecessarily angered. Positively, Paul also noted the father's role in caring for and guiding the development of children in their relationship with the Lord. This spiritual dimension is still often overlooked in our world.

Slaves and Masters (6:5–9)

In every one of these five verses, the spiritual dimension is mentioned. Notice the phrases: "obey Christ," "slaves of Christ," "doing the will of God," "serving the Lord," and "their Master and yours in heaven." In the secular law of the day, the slave had few rights; however in the Christian faith, both the slave and the master had a relationship with and in Christ that gave them common ground in their relationship with each other. This Scripture provided instructions for Christian living in relation to the institution of slavery in that day, but the whole body of New Testament teaching would eventually lead to condemnation of slavery.

In understanding Paul's words concerning slaves, we see implications for how we work in secular jobs and in the church. Although we may not have "earthly masters" as slaves had masters (6:5), we do know the importance of following instructions and doing the job for which we are paid or for which we have volunteered. We see the value of doing the job well, even if no one is looking (6:6). One motivation for that is that all work can be dedicated to God; thus, we want to please God in the workplace or in the church (6:6–7). The promise for good work is that God blesses and rewards the labor of the worker (6:8).

The most demanding word in 6:5–9 is seen in Paul's admonition to masters. Some masters were Christians, such as we see in Paul's Letter to Philemon. Paul told masters that they had obligations to their slaves.

THE PRACTICE OF LOVE AT HOME

The youth of your church were on a retreat, and one of the girls began to cry. Her story included concerns that her parents were going to get a divorce, and she felt she had caused problems at home that had hurt her parent's relationship. She said, "I really think they love each other, but I want to help us all to live together better. How can I do that?" In the light of the different kinds of relationships mentioned in this lesson's Scripture, how would you respond?

That was not politically true in the secular society, but both the master and slave were in a new relationship if they were Christians: they were brothers and sisters in Christ. Masters were to treat slaves not as things but as people, without threat or intimidation, desiring to please God in the way they dealt with slaves. Both master and slave were equally important to God. Paul's treatment of slavery became part of the seedbed for the abolition of slavery centuries later.

Then and Now

Sometimes when I have led Bible studies with young people, I have asked them to finish this sentence: "You are what you are when you are _____ ." Usually someone stated these two words: "at home." If charity begins at home, certainly the Christian faith must impact our home life. Building marriages and homes that honor Christ, reflect Christ, and unite people around Christ are still great needs in our world today.

"Submit to one another out of reverence for Christ" is the guiding principle that was to shape Christians' understanding of wives and husbands, children and parents, and slaves and masters (5:21). The principle of submission is not popular in our world. We have been taught to assert ourselves, do our own thing, and have life our way. Mutual submission means a husband submits himself to his wife, even as the wife submits herself to her husband. Such mutual submission is done on the highest motivation, "out of reverence for Christ." Reverence for Christ also affects everyone else in the home. However one interprets this lesson's Scripture, Paul established a principle that challenged the first century and continues to challenge the twenty-first century: "Submit to one another out of reverence for Christ."

QUESTIONS

1. What does "reverence for Christ" mean to you?

2. If you could change how you live in your family, what would you do differently?

3. How can your church do a more effective job of building up marriage and family life?

4. How do Paul's instructions concerning slaves and masters impact workplace relationships today?

5. How does this Scripture passage speak to single people and to married couples who have no children?

6. How does "there is no favoritism" (Eph. 6:9) or partiality on God's part affect the way you live?

Introducing

1 AND 2 TIMOTHY:
Leading the Church

Although 1 and 2 Timothy are different in character from each other, each in its own way provides instructions for Christian leadership. The emphasis of each is on care for the church's welfare. Along with the Letter to Titus, 1 and 2 Timothy have been called the *pastoral epistles* since the early eighteenth century. The name indicates that these letters are about providing care in a pastoral manner to the church.

First Timothy is the longer of the two letters to Timothy. It contains motivation, guidance, and encouragement for caring for the church. A special emphasis in this letter is on dealing with the challenge of "strange doctrines" (1 Timothy 1:3).[1] Misplaced doctrinal emphases and blatantly false teachings often threatened the early church's ministry, including the church at Ephesus where Timothy served (1 Tim. 1:3). The letter is written as a set of instructions for Timothy to know how to help the church in the challenges it faced. Timothy was younger and less experienced in guiding churches than was Paul.

As with 1 Timothy, 2 Timothy is identified as being from Paul to Timothy (2 Timothy 1:1–2). Rather than being a manual, a set of instructions, to use in guiding a church, this letter has more of a personal touch and reads like a legacy being left by an older mentor to a younger person. The legacy includes encouragement ("be strong in the grace that is in Christ Jesus," 2 Tim. 2:1) as well as instruction ("the things which you have heard from me in the presence of many witnesses, entrust these to faithful men who will be able to teach others also," 2:2).

These lessons from 1 and 2 Timothy about caring for the church as church leaders complement the lessons from Ephesians on the nature and mission of the church. As you study these Scriptures, look for ways to apply them to your life whether or not you consider yourself a church leader.

1 AND 2 TIMOTHY: LEADING THE CHURCH

Lesson 8	An Example to Follow	1 Timothy 1:1–5, 12–19
Lesson 9	Qualities of Worthy Church Leaders	1 Timothy 3:1–13
Lesson 10	Train for Godliness	1 Timothy 4
Lesson 11	God or Money?	1 Timothy 6:3–19
Lesson 12	Wake Up and Keep Going	2 Timothy 1:6–14; 2:1–15
Lesson 13	Toward a Future Filled with Hope	2 Timothy 4:1–8, 16–18

Additional Resources for Studying 1 and 2 Timothy[2]

James D. G. Dunn. "The First and Second Letters to Timothy and the Letter to Titus." *The New Interpreter's Bible*. Volume XI. Nashville, Tennessee: Abingdon Press, 2000.

Gordon D. Fee. *1 and 2 Timothy*. New International Biblical Commentary. Peabody, Massachusetts: Hendrickson Publishers, 1988.

Frank E. Gaebelin, general editor. "Ephesians—Philemon." *The Expositor's Bible Commentary*. Grand Rapids, Michigan: Zondervan, 1978.

W. Hulitt Gloer. *1 & 2 Timothy, Titus*. Smyth & Helwys Bible Commentary. Volume 29a. Macon, Georgia: Smyth & Helwys Publishing, 2010.

Donald Guthrie. *The Pastoral Epistles*. Revised edition. Tyndale New Testament Commentaries. Grand Rapids, Michigan: William B. Eerdmans Publishing Company, 1990.

E. Glenn Hinson. "1—2 Timothy and Titus." *The Broadman Bible Commentary*. Volume 11. Nashville, Tennessee: Broadman Press, 1971.

Craig S. Keener. *IVP Bible Background Commentary: New Testament.* Downers Grove, Illinois: InterVarsity Press, 1993.

Tremper Longman III and David E. Garland, general editors. "Ephesians—Philemon." *The Expositor's Bible Commentary, Revised Edition,* Volume 12. Grand Rapids, Michigan, Zondervan, 2006.

George W. Knight III. *Commentary on the Pastoral Epistles.* New International Greek Testament Commentary. Grand Rapids, Michigan: William B. Eerdmans Publishing Company, 1992.

Thomas D. Lea and Hayne P. Griffin, Jr. *1, 2 Timothy, Titus.* The New American Commentary. Volume 34. Nashville, Tennessee: Broadman Press, 1992.

Walter L. Liefeld. *1 & 2 Timothy/Titus.* The NIV Application Commentary. Grand Rapids, Michigan: Zondervan, 1999.

William D. Mounce. *Pastoral Epistles.* Word Biblical Commentary. Nashville, Tennessee: Thomas Nelson, 1982.

The New Interpreter's Study Bible. Nashville, Tennessee: Abingdon Press, 2003.

A.T. Robertson. *Word Pictures in the New Testament.* Volume IV. Nashville, Tennessee: Broadman Press, 1931.

John R. W. Stott. *Guard the Gospel: The Message of 2 Timothy.* Downers Grove, Illinois: InterVarsity Press, 1973.

NOTES

1. Unless otherwise indicated, all Scripture quotations in "Introducing 1 and 2 Timothy: Leading the Church" are from the New American Standard Bible (1995 edition).

2. Listing a book does not imply full agreement by the writers or BAPTISTWAY PRESS® with all of its comments.

FOCAL TEXT
1 Timothy 1:1–5, 12–19

BACKGROUND
1 Timothy 1

MAIN IDEA

Paul's experience of God's grace and mercy shaped his life, his ministry, and his message, and provided an example of leadership and service for Timothy.

QUESTIONS TO EXPLORE

Who has provided for you a positive example of Christian leadership and service? How are you providing such an example to others?

STUDY AIM

To identify qualities of Paul that provide an example of Christian leadership and service worth following

QUICK READ

Serving and leading in the Christian faith can sometimes be difficult as one faces questions of credibility as well as opposition from false teachers. Especially in these times, God's grace and mercy should shape our ministries.

LESSON EIGHT

An Example to Follow

When I first shared a sense of calling to the gospel ministry with some friends in college, their reaction was one of disbelief and fear. First, they wondered how I could be called to preach when I was just like them—the same kind of sinner. Second, they were afraid I would become too religious to be their friend. But through prayer, the study of Scripture, and wise counsel, I have been serving as a pastor confidently now for forty-five years.[1]

1 TIMOTHY 1:1–5, 12–19

[1] Paul, an apostle of Christ Jesus by the command of God our Savior and of Christ Jesus our hope, [2] To Timothy my true son in the faith: Grace, mercy and peace from God the Father and Christ Jesus our Lord.

[3] As I urged you when I went into Macedonia, stay there in Ephesus so that you may command certain men not to teach false doctrines any longer [4] nor to devote themselves to myths and endless genealogies. These promote controversies rather than God's work—which is by faith. [5] The goal of this command is love, which comes from a pure heart and a good conscience and a sincere faith.

• •

[12] I thank Christ Jesus our Lord, who has given me strength, that he considered me faithful, appointing me to his service. [13] Even though I was once a blasphemer and a persecutor and a violent man, I was shown mercy because I acted in ignorance and unbelief. [14] The grace of our Lord was poured out on me abundantly, along with the faith and love that are in Christ Jesus. [15] Here is a trustworthy saying that deserves full acceptance: Christ Jesus came into the world to save sinners—of whom I am the worst. [16] But for that very reason I was shown mercy so that in me, the worst of sinners, Christ Jesus might display his unlimited patience as an example for those who would believe on him and receive eternal life. [17] Now to the King eternal, immortal, invisible, the only God, be honor and glory for ever and ever. Amen. [18] Timothy, my son, I give you this instruction in keeping with the prophecies

once made about you, so that by following them you may fight the good fight, [19] holding on to faith and a good conscience. Some have rejected these and so have shipwrecked their faith.

Paul Was Confident of His Call (1:1–2)

Paul asserted that he was an apostle of Christ Jesus by the command of God and of Jesus Christ. In saying this, Paul was acknowledging what was already known of him. That is, he was not chosen as one of the twelve apostles after the death of Judas, one of the apostles chosen originally by Jesus Christ. In fact, the eleven surviving apostles had chosen a man named Matthias to replace Judas as one of the twelve. They were specific about the one who should be chosen. "Therefore it is necessary to choose one of the men who have been with us the whole time the Lord Jesus went in and out among us, beginning with John's baptism to the time when Jesus was taken up from us. For one of these must become a witness with us of his resurrection" (Acts 1:21–22). Paul did not fit this condition.

In fact, Paul had been a persecutor of those who had followed Jesus Christ. But when God called Paul by his grace so that he might preach, Paul "did not consult any man" (Galatians 1:13). So, Paul did not have a pedigree. Paul did not have a personal relationship with the physical and earthly Jesus, and Paul was not on the inside of the apostolic group.

Yet Paul was confident of his calling because of his personal encounter with the Lord Jesus Christ. Paul's encounter with Jesus is recorded in Acts 9 (see also Acts 22; 26). Paul was on the road to Damascus to persecute and imprison followers of Jesus when Jesus personally confronted him with the question, "Saul, Saul, why do you persecute me?" (Acts 9:4). Paul asked, "Who are you, Lord?" (Acts 9:5). Jesus replied, "I am Jesus, whom you are persecuting. Now get up and go into the city, and you will be told what you must do" (Acts 9:5). From that point on Paul's confidence in his calling was secure. He was serving at the command of God and Jesus Christ.

Paul's leadership began with his confidence in a personal relationship with Jesus Christ and personal calling from Jesus Christ. Any effective Christian leader needs a strong and confident knowledge of a personal relationship with Jesus Christ and a personal calling to do Christ's work.

Paul Was Courageous in the Face of Opposition (1:3–4, 18–19)

Paul had left Timothy in Ephesus and had traveled on to Macedonia, where several years earlier he had gone following the vision at Troas (Acts 16:9). Ephesus was the chief major city of Asia Minor, the seat of the governor or proconsul of the province. It was the location of the famous temple of Artemis, or Diana (Acts 19:23–28). Paul, Apollos, Aquila, Priscilla, and Timothy ministered there. Ephesus is located today in modern Turkey. The church in Ephesus was surrounded by many pagan religions and was battling to maintain its message.

Ministry in Ephesus was challenging. Timothy faced withering opposition from those who worshiped false gods and from "certain men" who "teach false doctrines . . . and devote themselves to myths and endless genealogies. These promote controversies rather than God's work . . ." (1 Timothy 1:3–4).

Who were these "certain men," and what were their "false doctrines"? Paul did not name the "certain men" unless they were "Hymenaeus and Alexander," named in 1 Timothy 1:20. Some commentators believe the term "certain men" simply meant that there were several men who were teaching false doctrines. Paul referred to these heretics by the impersonal "some" (1 Tim. 1:6, 19).

Paul accused these "certain men" of teaching "false doctrine," "myths and endless genealogies." The Greek verb translated "teach false doctrine" is rare, occurring in the New Testament only in 1 Timothy 1:3 and 6:3. The content of their "false doctrines" was "myths and genealogies." The "myths" were fables or stories about gods, and Paul labeled them as "false." Many of these myths were told to lend credence to immoral behavior linked to stories of ancient gods.

The "genealogies" could have been linked to Israel's history, giving these teachers a sense of false piety in connection with past leaders. Paul labeled them "endless," which could have meant *pointless, inconclusive,* or *contradictory.* It is clear that Paul considered this linkage to earlier leaders as deceptive and dangerous.

Paul told Timothy to "command certain men not to teach false doctrines any longer" (1:3) The word "command" carried with it the authority Paul felt was his as an apostle from God and Jesus Christ. He encouraged Timothy to "fight the good fight, holding onto faith and a good conscience" (1:18–19).

A Christian leader has to be courageous in the face of "false doctrine" or "pointless credentials" presented by those who seek to dilute or destroy the Christian faith. The authority for this courage comes from Jesus Christ through the Scriptures.

Paul Was Compassionate in His Teaching (1:5)

Even as Paul commanded Timothy to be firm with those who were trying to pervert the gospel, he also pointed out to Timothy the purpose of this command. "The goal of this command is love, which comes from a pure heart and a good conscience and a sincere faith" (1:5).

The Scriptures remind us that "God is love" (1 John 4:16). Jesus taught that loving God and loving others is the greatest commandment (Matthew 22:37–38). So what Paul told Timothy was something Paul

TIMOTHY

In Acts 16:1–3, we read of Paul's selection of Timothy to be one of his coworkers. Acts tells us that Timothy's mother was "a Jewess and a believer," but his father was "a Greek." In 2 Timothy 1:5, we learn of Timothy's "sincere faith, which first lived in your grandmother Lois and in your mother Eunice. . . ." Further, Paul wrote in 2 Timothy 3:15 that Timothy knew the Scriptures "from infancy."

Part of the reason Paul chose Timothy as a coworker is because "the brothers at Lystra and Iconium spoke well of him" (Acts 16:2). Later Paul would say that Timothy "proved himself" by serving alongside Paul in proclaiming the gospel (Philippians 2:22). Paul proclaimed his love for Timothy as one who is "faithful in the Lord" (1 Corinthians 4:17). Paul praised Timothy for continuing to serve Christ effectively, "carrying on the work of the Lord" (1 Corinthians 16:10).

learned firsthand in his relationship with Jesus Christ when the grace of God was "poured out" on him (1 Tim. 1:14).

Paul pointed out to Timothy that the threefold source of love is "a pure heart and a good conscience and a sincere faith" (1:5). Look at each of these. First, love comes from a "pure heart." The heart is the location of human personality and the origin of human emotions and intentions (Matt. 15:19). It is with the heart that people relate to God and others. Second, love is produced by "a good conscience." The conscience is the will that moves a person from correct doctrine to correct behavior. It is the inner messenger that instructs one to behave in the proper way. This love is also produced by "a sincere faith." This phrase points to an authentic and consistent lifestyle proceeding from one's belief in the gospel. It is the opposite lifestyle of the false or deceptive teachers. Love produces a pure or clean heart, which in turn produces a good conscience and a sincere faith.

Timothy was to teach all those listening, including those teaching "myths and endless genealogies," that the gospel produces something that these "myths and endless genealogies" will never produce—love, a pure heart, a good conscience, and a sincere faith.

Paul Was Convinced of His Salvation (1:12–17)

Paul did not try to convince people of his apostolic authority as a teacher based on his past life and achievements. Instead he pointed out that his gratefulness for the apostolic call came from the grace and mercy of Jesus "poured out on me abundantly along with the faith and love that are in Christ Jesus" (1 Tim. 1:14).

Had Paul tried to stand in his own strength, he would have failed completely. He was "once a blasphemer and a persecutor and a violent man" (1:13). In fact, while Stephen was being stoned by an angry crowd of religious leaders, Paul stood by watching and giving approval (Acts 8:1). That is not a great testimony on which to build a respectable Christian life or to inspire faithful leadership.

Paul gave God credit for giving him the strength to continue carrying the gospel to the world. He was always amazed that God would consider him faithful, appointing him to God's service. Paul could never have been as effective in proclaiming the gospel of Jesus Christ had he not

---

CASE STUDY

Several years ago a Baptist church wanted to initiate a stronger singles ministry. The one that had been meeting at the church never had more than six or seven in attendance. A young adult man had recently professed his faith in Jesus and had been baptized. He had been divorced but had remarried and now had two children. He was managing a restaurant that served alcoholic beverages.

After becoming a Christian, he wanted to get out of the restaurant business and get another job. But in the meantime he began to work with the singles in the church. Within a year the singles group had more than a hundred singles in attendance every Sunday under his leadership, with many of them professing their faith and being baptized. An older church leader came to the pastor and wanted this young man removed because of his past life. If you were the pastor, what would you do?

---

experienced the grace of God in his life personally.

Paul reinforced his own conversion and call to ministry by this statement: "Here is a trustworthy saying" (a saying that has weight to it or reliability to it) "that deserves full acceptance:" (it is so important that it should be accepted by all who hear it) "Christ Jesus came into the world to save sinners—of whom I am the worst" (1 Tim. 1:15).

Then Paul reminded Timothy that what God did for him God would do for others who believe (1:16). Paul was a display of the "unlimited patience" of Christ Jesus toward sinners (1:16).

Every Christian leader should remember that it is God's mercy and grace that gives one the strength to lead. Not one person deserves the mercy and grace of God. It comes to each one through the sacrificial death and resurrection of the Lord Jesus Christ.

Implications and Actions

By God's grace and mercy, Paul overcame a horrible background to become one of the great leaders and teachers of the Christian faith. Despite his past, the grace of God gave him the courage to confront false teachers in love and to remain faithful to the pure gospel of Jesus Christ. He never soft-pedaled the gospel or shrank back in fear because of his past. He was convinced that Jesus could save anyone since he—"the worst" of all sinners—was saved by God's grace.

The same grace and mercy of God is available to each one of us today. Through this grace and mercy, we can receive the confidence, courage, compassion and conviction to be an effective Christian servant and leader.

QUESTIONS

1. What part of your life takes away the confidence you should have as a Christian leader?

2. How do you respond biblically to someone who brings up some part of your past that is not honoring to God?

3. What is your most effective tactic for confronting false teachers?

4. How do you show love to those who are not teaching a pure gospel?

NOTES

1. Unless otherwise indicated, all Scripture quotations in lessons 1–13 are from the New International Version (1984 edition).

FOCAL TEXT
1 Timothy 3:1–13

BACKGROUND
1 Timothy 3:1–13

MAIN IDEA
Church leaders are to be people of high spiritual qualifications who care faithfully for God's church and serve and represent it well.

QUESTION TO EXPLORE
What should we look for in church leaders?

STUDY AIM
To summarize the instructions about church leaders and list implications for my church's leadership practices

QUICK READ
The most effective church leadership is centered in people with strong character who serve the church faithfully and represent it well.

Who comes to mind when you think of worthy church leadership? Two people come to my mind. One is my childhood pastor, and the other is my father-in-law. My pastor would be considered an overseer or an elder, and my father-in-law was a deacon. Both men had gentle spirits, strong families, and strong character. They served the church family well. My father-in-law is still active in his church at more than ninety years of age.

1 TIMOTHY 3:1–13

1 Here is a trustworthy saying: If anyone sets his heart on being an overseer, he desires a noble task. 2 Now the overseer must be above reproach, the husband of but one wife, temperate, self-controlled, respectable, hospitable, able to teach, 3 not given to drunkenness, not violent but gentle, not quarrelsome, not a lover of money. 4 He must manage his own family well and see that his children obey him with proper respect. 5 (If anyone does not know how to manage his own family, how can he take care of God's church?) 6 He must not be a recent convert, or he may become conceited and fall under the same judgment as the devil. 7 He must also have a good reputation with outsiders, so that he will not fall into disgrace and into the devil's trap. 8 Deacons, likewise, are to be men worthy of respect, sincere, not indulging in much wine, and not pursuing dishonest gain. 9 They must keep hold of the deep truths of the faith with a clear conscience. 10 They must first be tested; and then if there is nothing against them, let them serve as deacons. 11 In the same way, their wives are to be women worthy of respect, not malicious talkers but temperate and trustworthy in everything. 12 A deacon must be the husband of but one wife and must manage his children and his household well. 13 Those who have served well gain an excellent standing and great assurance in their faith in Christ Jesus.

Leadership in the Church Is a Worthy Task (3:1)

This part of Paul's letter begins with his second "trustworthy" saying (1 Timothy 1:15; 3:1). What Paul was saying had special significance for the church and was to be accepted as true or "trustworthy." Paul was calling for the full attention of his readers to what followed. What was it that needed the full attention of these readers?

It was the desire to be an "overseer" or leader in the church. Whatever the setting in which a church ministered, each church needed an "overseer," a leader.

When Paul said that one "sets his heart on being an overseer," did he mean that being an "overseer" was a worthy ambition? Was it a leadership position someone sought, or was it a leadership position to which someone was appointed, either by people or by God? In Paul's case, his leadership position came from a divine appointment. He said that God *appointed* him to service (1 Tim. 1:12).

In the case of the "overseers" in Ephesus, it was the Holy Spirit who appointed them over the churches (Acts 20:28). In the case of elders in the first century, it appears that in some cases they were appointed by the apostles (Acts 14:23; Titus 1:5).

Both the overseer and the deacon were to be people who "manage" their own families well (1 Tim. 3:4, 12). What does it mean to "manage" one's family and one's church well?

The Greek verb used in 1 Timothy 3:4 and 3:12 for "manage" is *proistamai*. It is used also to describe leading in the church in 1 Timothy 5:17 and Romans 12:8. It literally means *to stand before* or *to lead*. It implies *to care for*.

So a person who does not stand before his or her family to lead or to care for them is not fit to stand before the church family to lead or care for them. The word translated in 1 Timothy 3:5 as "take care of" is a compound Greek word meaning to *exercise concern for*. It means to give leadership and guidance to family as well as church family.

Does this mean that a single person or a childless person cannot be considered to be an overseer or a deacon? Certainly not! It simply means that those with families must manage them well.

Therefore, if a person senses that God is calling him or her to be an overseer or a deacon, and that person has a family, the person must confront the issue of family management. First take care of the family, and then answer God's call to take care of the church family. Leadership in the church is a noble or worthy task.

Leadership in the Church Requires Worthy Character (3:2–12)

The importance of the task of leadership for an overseer or a deacon determines the focus of the rest of the leadership attributes. Each leadership role is regarded from the standpoint of qualifications and not duties. Therefore, Paul's stress is on the quality of the leader's character, although suitable spiritual gifts and abilities would be assumed from Paul's writings in 1 Corinthians 12. There is a good deal of overlap in the qualities required for both overseer and deacon, but the same general quality holds true for both—a blameless reputation.

Paul began his description of the qualities of an overseer with these words, "Now the overseer must be . . ." (1 Tim. 3:2). Paul used the Greek word translated "must" twice in verses 2–12 (3:2, 7) and implied it several more times so that the New International Version has "must" in 1 Timothy 3:4, 6, 9, 10, and 12 (twice) in addition. The word "must" emphasizes the urgent importance of these qualities for effective leadership in the church.

At the head of the list of qualifications for an overseer is the term "above reproach" (3:2), signaling that the overseer's observable behavior must be without blame. The overseer must have a good reputation among all people.

In my lifetime, I have known some wonderful pastors and wonderful deacons, and I've known some mean pastors and mean deacons. These mean people were obviously missing the first requirement for effective church leadership.

Paul began his list of characteristics for the overseer with six positive attributes. The first attribute addresses the overseer's marriage. The Greek expression translated "husband of but one wife" (3:2, 12) means that the overseer (as well as the deacon) is not to be a polygamist.[1] Interpreters also comment that the phrase calls for faithfulness to one's wife. Second, the overseer is to be "temperate" or balanced. The church does not need loose cannons in leadership. Third, the overseer is to be "self-controlled." The overseer should not be one who is overcome by passions. The overseer should be "prudent" (NASB). Fourth, the overseer must be "respectable." Respect is earned by one's behavior. If a person's behavior is rude or disrespectful, then that person should not be in leadership. Fifth, the overseer must be "hospitable," with the gift of relating to people. The overseer must like people. I've known overseers, pastors, who did not like being around people. They were good on the platform but horrible around people off the platform. They were not afraid of crowds but were afraid of individuals.

After Paul listed these qualities, he mixed some prohibitions with them: "not given to drunkenness, not violent but gentle, not quarrelsome, not a lover of money." When Paul wrote, "not a lover of money," we do well to think of 1 Timothy 6:10, "For the love of money is a root of all kinds of evil." Otherwise good and decent leaders have been ruined by the love of money.

I served as pastor of a church years ago that had in leadership a man with a violent temper. He would get his way in meetings by blowing up in anger at anyone who opposed his ideas. The sad story was that the other leaders in the church would not confront this deacon and make him deal with his problem. He should never have been selected to lead. When I asked some of the other leaders of the church to help

FAMILY AND LEADERSHIP

Managing one's family is the most important Christian stewardship in life. Paul makes managing one's family one of the main qualities of the life of the overseer and deacon. In fact, in 1 Timothy 5:8, Paul wrote that one who "does not provide for his relatives, and especially for his immediate family . . . has denied the faith and is worse than an unbeliever." This word "provides" is from the Greek word *pronoei*, which is a compound word composed of *pro*, meaning *before*, and *noeo*, meaning *to think*. To provide is to think ahead about how to care for the family. The family is not to be an afterthought.

Unfortunately many people involved in church leadership as overseers and deacons make the church family their first thought and their nuclear family an afterthought. This is one of the reasons overseers and deacons sometimes do not manage their families well. A family that is not cared for well will become a liability for any person's ministry. A church filled with mismanaged families will be a mismanaged church. A wise Christian woman was asked one day what Christians could do to promote world peace. She answered, "Go home and love your family."

me deal with this man's problem, their answer to me was: "You will be gone one day, but we have to live here with him." And you know what? They were right.

Overseers must be able to manage their own families well in order to be able to manage the church family well. An overseer must not be "a recent convert." The danger of being a recent convert was that the leader might "become conceited and fall under the same judgment as the devil." The overseer might try to take the place of God.

Paul began listing the qualifications of deacons with the same kind of statement he made in reference to overseers. Deacons were to be "worthy of respect," and in the same way the wives or women deacons were to be "women worthy of respect." More than eighty years ago, A.T. Robertson, generally considered to be Baptists' greatest Greek scholar, wrote these words about the phrase translated "women worthy of respect": "Apparently 'women as deacons' (Romans 16:1 about Phoebe) and not women in general or just 'wives of deacons.'"[2]

In addition to many of the same personal characteristics of the overseer, these are added to the deacon: keeping "hold of the deep truths of the faith with a clear conscience" and first being "tested" to see that "there is nothing against them." Being literate in Christian teachings and being tested were essential to the selection of the early deacons. One additional qualification was added for deacons' wives or women deacons: do not be "malicious talkers." I don't know why Paul addressed this just to women. The same prohibition should be made for the men as well.

Leadership in the Church Is Rewarded with Worthy Assurances (3:13)

Paul emphasized that those who "have served well" would be strengthened in their stature in the community and in their faith in Jesus Christ. They would have a strong reputation in the church family and would have strong confidence in their faith in Jesus Christ. They would be spiritually solid. This is a twofold reward for faithful leadership in the church. These two commendations were lacking in the lives of the false teachers mentioned by Paul in 1 Timothy 1:19.

In most Baptist churches today leadership resides in the pastor, the staff, the deacons, and various organizations and committees. Pastors in

---

TIRED AND BURNED OUT

Some years ago a pastor and friend resigned a prestigious pulpit in a large metropolitan area. This pastor was very gifted as a preacher and leader. He was visionary and energetic. But he wrote to his congregation these words: "I am tired and burned out—no good to myself or to anyone else." If you had ten minutes with this pastor, what would you say to help him recover?

---

the typical Baptist church would be similar to the overseer and elder in the New Testament church. In fact, the words "overseers" and "elders" are used interchangeably in Acts 20:17, 28 and Titus 1:5, 7. Staff members in some Baptist churches are considered as elders, such as teaching elders, music elders, etc. The pastor is considered the ruling elder.

Three Greek words are used to describe the pastoral leadership of the New Testament church: *episcopos*—translated *overseer* or *bishop; presbuteros*—translated *elder*; and *poimen*—translated *shepherd* or *pastor*. In most Baptist churches, the pastor would wear all three hats. However, the pastor may delegate teaching and pastoral responsibilities to other staff members.

The deacon in a Baptist church is seen as a leader in ministry to the congregation. The model for deacon ministry comes from the appointment of seven men in Acts 6:1–6 to care for the needs of the widows in the daily distribution of food in the early church and to put down grumbling in the church. Their entire focus was and is to be servant ministry. Deacons were not and are not called or appointed to run the church. The Greek word *diakonos* is translated *servant*.

Oversight and ministry in the local church, whether by overseer or deacon, makes a valuable contribution to the life of the congregation and brings honor to the leaders.

Implications and Actions

In the first century the Christian faith was in its infancy. The early believers did not have the benefit of a printed New Testament to reinforce what they believed. It was essential that the church have strong leaders to care for them and guide them in Christian doctrine and behavior. The danger of false teachers was always lurking near these early believers.

Even though we have our Bible, Old and New Testaments, in print today, there is still a vital need for leadership in the New Testament church. This need for leadership involves taking care of and leading the church family. Is God calling you to become involved in leadership as an overseer or deacon?

QUESTIONS

1. What quality do you think is most important for leadership in the church today?

2. What quality do you think is missing in much of our church leadership today?

3. What quality do you admire the most in your overseer or pastor today?

4. What do your deacons do best to serve your church family?

NOTES

1. "One woman at a time," states Greek scholar A.T. Robertson in *Word Pictures in the New Testament*, vol. IV (Nashville, Tennessee: Broadman Press, 1931), 572.

2. Robertson, *Word Pictures in the New Testament*, vol. IV, 575, on 1 Timothy 3:11.

MAIN IDEA

Paul instructed Timothy to train himself for godliness in order to ensure his own spiritual welfare and also to be prepared to lead others to walk in that way themselves.

QUESTION TO EXPLORE

In what ways do you intentionally seek to train yourself for godliness?

STUDY AIM

To identify specific ways for training myself for godliness and decide on at least one I will put into practice

QUICK READ

As physical fitness trainers need to train to take care of their own health and be prepared to instruct others in taking care of their health, Christians need to train in godliness for their own spiritual welfare and to be able to lead others to walk in the Christian way.

LESSON TEN
Train for Godliness

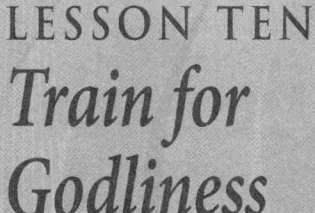

One of the football coaches I worked with when I was a student at the University of Arkansas was the legendary Baltimore Colts wide receiver Raymond Berry. Coach Berry was a dedicated Christian who took every opportunity to share Christ with others. Through his witness a number of coaches accepted Christ.

One of the things that made Coach Berry so effective was his Scripture memory plan. He carried around with him Scripture printed on three-by-five cards. During the day I would see him walking around looking at those cards as he memorized Scripture. He was training himself so that he would be spiritually healthy and capable of training others in spiritual disciplines.

1 TIMOTHY 4

¹ The Spirit clearly says that in later times some will abandon the faith and follow deceiving spirits and things taught by demons. ² Such teachings come through hypocritical liars, whose consciences have been seared as with a hot iron. ³ They forbid people to marry and order them to abstain from certain foods, which God created to be received with thanksgiving by those who believe and who know the truth. ⁴ For everything God created is good, and nothing is to be rejected if it is received with thanksgiving, ⁵ because it is consecrated by the word of God and prayer. ⁶ If you point these things out to the brothers, you will be a good minister of Christ Jesus, brought up in the truths of the faith and of the good teaching that you have followed. ⁷ Have nothing to do with godless myths and old wives' tales; rather, train yourself to be godly. ⁸ For physical training is of some value, but godliness has value for all things, holding promise for both the present life and the life to come. ⁹ This is a trustworthy saying that deserves full acceptance ¹⁰ (and for this we labor and strive), that we have put our hope in the living God, who is the Savior of all men, and especially of those who believe. ¹¹ Command and teach these things. ¹² Don't let anyone look down on you because you are young, but set an example for the believers in speech, in life, in love, in faith and in purity. ¹³ Until I come, devote yourself to the public reading of Scripture, to preaching and to teaching. ¹⁴ Do

not neglect your gift, which was given you through a prophetic message when the body of elders laid their hands on you. [15] Be diligent in these matters; give yourself wholly to them, so that everyone may see your progress. [16] Watch your life and doctrine closely. Persevere in them, because if you do, you will save both yourself and your hearers.

Resistance Training (4:1–6)

A key element in training for godliness is to resist those things that would be detrimental to health and growth. The older we get the more difficult it may be to resist those things that are not good for us.

Consider that thought in relation to the phrase, "in later times" (1 Timothy 4:1). Eugene Peterson in *The Message* version of the New Testament renders this phrase "as time goes on."

The first-century church was familiar with the Jewish idea of time. Time was divided into two stages—this present age, which is bad and will get worse because it is in the grip of evil powers; and the age to come, which is the golden age of God's reign in his newly created world.

It is in these "later times" that people get lazy, not maintaining spiritual discipline, and thus wander away from the faith to follow "deceiving spirits." Paul referred to these folks as people with "itching ears" who would not put up with "sound doctrine" (2 Timothy 4:3).

Paul said these spiritually lazy people would follow teachers who were "hypocritical liars, whose consciences have been seared as with a hot iron." Sometimes we resist telling the truth about religious leaders in our own day who fit the description of these first-century charlatans, but they are around us no less. We must develop resistance training to confront their false teaching.

The false teachers to which Paul referred spoke directly against God's word in forbidding people "to marry and order them to abstain from certain foods" (1 Tim. 4:3). They spoke against what God proclaimed in Genesis 2:18, "The LORD God said, 'It is not good for the man to be alone. I will make a helper suitable for him." They spoke against what God said in Genesis 1:31, that everything God had created was "very good." Paul wrote in Romans 14:17, "For the kingdom of God is not a matter of eating and drinking, but of righteousness, peace and joy in the Holy Spirit."

Paul reminded Timothy not to be misled by this outward legalistic behavior but to receive everything from God with thanksgiving, realizing that all creation is "consecrated by the word of God and prayer" (1 Tim. 4:5). It's easy to put on an outward show of godliness, but it requires discipline to continue in the faithful study of God's word and in prayer.

Strength Training (4:7–11)

Strength training means avoiding those things that *will not* build strength and including those things that *will* build strength. "Godless myths and old wives' tales" were two things Paul warned Timothy to avoid. The Greek word for "have nothing to do with," *paraiteomai*, is an imperative or command. Paul was using strong language so that Timothy would understand that these were things to strictly avoid or reject. We must pay close attention to what these two things represent because they are present in our day as well.

"Myths" were made-up stories with no grounding in biblical truth. The word "myths" suggests they were like tales older women would tell young children—made-up stories that did not have to be truthful. Some scholars believe that Paul was using a sarcastic term used in philosophical polemic to compare an opponent's position to tales told by older women while sitting around doing nothing constructive.

Do we have people who spread "godless myths and old wives' tales" in the religious world today? Absolutely! Teachers who remake the scriptural plan of salvation, which is based on faith in Jesus Christ alone, so as to allow for any and all beliefs and messiahs in order to be forgiven of sin and go to heaven are guilty of telling godless myths. Teachers who promise that following Jesus Christ will make one wealthy and healthy for life are spinning "old wives' tales." It is as urgent in our day, in these "later times," as it was in Timothy's day to "have nothing to do with godless myths and old wives' tales."

Instead, we should train ourselves to be godly. Just as we train our bodies for strength and health, we should train our souls for spiritual strength and health. Training our bodies is good for this life, but time

THE SAVIOR OF ALL PEOPLE

What did Paul mean when he said in 1 Timothy 4:10, "the living God, who is the Savior of all men, and especially of those who believe"? What did Paul mean when he said in 1 Timothy 2:3–4, "This is good and pleases God our Savior who wants all men to be saved and to come to a knowledge of the truth"? Recall, too, that Peter wrote, "The Lord is not slow in keeping his promise as some understand slowness. He is patient with you, not wanting anyone to perish, but everyone to come to repentance" (2 Peter 3:9).

To say that God wants all people to be saved or that God is the Savior of all people does not imply that all people will be saved. The Scriptures are clear that it is those who believe who will be saved. "Salvation is found in no one else, for there is no other name under heaven given to men by which we must be saved" (Acts 4:12).

and age will eventually wear them out no matter how well we train. But training ourselves to be godly will last not only for this life but for eternity. Peter wrote that God "in his great mercy . . . has given us new birth into a living hope through the resurrection of Jesus Christ from the dead, and into an inheritance that can never perish, spoil or fade . . ." (1 Peter 1:3–4).

Our strength training comes from our "hope in the living God, who is the Savior of all men, and especially of those who believe" (1 Tim. 4:10).

Core Training (4:12–16)

Any good physical fitness trainer will be certain that the core muscles are worked on regularly because it is these core muscles that support every other muscle. A physically fit person needs strong abdominal muscles, strong back muscles, and strong chest muscles. It is this core that feeds every other muscle group.

Spiritual fitness demands that core training be done for godliness beginning with a good example. No matter whether a person is young or old in chronological age or in spiritual age, a godly example is hard to refute. A godly example in the life of a young believer is especially

SOME SPIRITUAL EXERCISES

1. Identify one religious group in America today that would fit the *godless myth* category, and use Scripture to refute their teachings.

2. Explain why some Christian groups abstain from marrying or eating certain foods.

3. Keep a journal for one week detailing how you set an example for other believers "in speech, in life, in love, in faith and in purity" (1 Tim. 4:12).

4. Find three Scriptures that teach salvation by faith alone, and write a brief explanation of how they refute the notion that everyone will ultimately be saved.

powerful. It is hard for anyone to "look down on" a young believer who has a powerful example. A godly example is a testimony to the training that has been taking place in one's core spiritual life. It is clear to see when it is an example "in speech, in life, in love, in faith and in purity" (4:12).

Added to the core of a godly example is the devotion to "the public reading of Scripture, to preaching, and to teaching" (4:13). Many of the newer churches today have given up on the public reading of Scripture, preaching, and teaching and instead rely almost exclusively on the novelty and entertainment of technology. One church in our area publishes their programs at the beginning of the year in a slick brochure. At the top of the first page of the brochure is the proclamation, "We Are Not A Sunday School Church." They announce right away that one can attend and not have to worry about a devotion to the study of the Scriptures. Another church sends out slick mailings proclaiming, "We have the best band in town." Nothing is ever said in any publication about Jesus or the Bible.

One of the churches in America that touts the largest attendance each week was told by their marketing experts to not put any religious symbols in or on their buildings so they wouldn't turn people away. So they put a globe and American flags all around the building. People who attend learn to worship power and success.

Paul warned Timothy to "watch your life and doctrine closely" (4:16). That can't be done without being devoted to the reading of Scripture.

The final core discipline Paul emphasized is that of spiritual gifting. Paul warned Timothy not to try to live the Christian life apart from his spiritual gift. This gift was "given you through a prophetic message when the body of elders laid their hands on you" (4:14). Does this mean that the elders actually conveyed the spiritual gift through their hands? It is God's Holy Spirit who gifts a person with special spiritual gifts (1 Corinthians 12:4–11). The message identifying Timothy's gift was given through a prophecy conveyed through elders by the Holy Spirit. There is no magic in one's hands to convey a spiritual gift. Putting their hands on Timothy meant that the elders recognized the spiritual gift Timothy had, and they put their hands on him to acknowledge that gift. Paul reminded Timothy of the same thought in 2 Timothy 1:6, ". . . I remind you to fan into the flame the gift of God, which is in you through the laying on of my hands." When Paul laid his hands on Timothy, he was commissioning Timothy to use the gift God gave him.

Paul ended this part of his instructions to Timothy by telling him, "Be diligent . . . give yourself wholly . . . persevere" (1 Tim. 4:15–16). Doing these things would lead to salvation for Timothy himself and for his hearers.

Implications and Actions

Training for godliness requires one to be completely devoted to Jesus Christ and the Scriptures. This devotion helps one resist deceiving spirits and hypocritical teachers. The value of godliness not only strengthens one for this life but also lasts into eternity.

Believers training for godliness will not be sidetracked by godless myths and meaningless tales but will remain strong in the truths of the faith. Their hope will be in the living God, and in that hope they will be saved. Believers training for godliness will set a good example and will lead others to set an example "in speech, in life, in love, in faith and in purity" (4:12). Believers training in righteousness will not neglect their spiritual gift but will give themselves completely and diligently in exercising that gift. As believers exercise their spiritual gift, they will lead others to do the same.

QUESTIONS

1. What godless myths identify spiritual charlatans today?

2. What religious groups do you know of today who for religious reasons forbid to marry or to abstain from certain foods?

3. What reasons do people give to try to justify that God will save all people no matter what they believe?

4. What is your spiritual gift? How are you using it?

God or Money?

FOCAL TEXT
1 Timothy 6:3–19

BACKGROUND
1 Timothy 6

MAIN IDEA
Christians must emphasize godliness rather than seeking material wealth and must use the wealth they have for God's purposes.

QUESTION TO EXPLORE
Is our attitude toward and use of our money truly Christlike?

STUDY AIM
To evaluate my attitude toward and use of money in light of this lesson's teachings about material wealth

QUICK READ
When people shape their money around themselves, they are following false doctrine. When they shape their money around God's good news, they are following sound doctrine.

The first church I served as pastor out of seminary was the Calvary Baptist Church in Little Rock, Arkansas. Because of our rapid growth, we decided to expand our sanctuary. We also decided that we would put a new Bible into every pew rack along with the hymnals. One man donated enough money for several hundred Bibles. We were very excited when the Bibles arrived and were placed into the pews.

Several weeks after the new Bibles were in the pews, I was preaching from 1 Timothy 6:3–10. I directed the congregation to the passage of Scripture and noted that if they wanted they could use the new pew Bibles. As I read from my Bible I could hear snickering in the congregation. It seems that a typographical error in the new Bibles caused 1 Timothy 6:6 to read, "But godliness with contentment is great *pain*" (italics added for emphasis).

I suppose the typo might have expressed the attitude of some Christians toward the biblical teachings about material wealth. The godly use of material wealth could be painful for many believers. But should it be?

1 TIMOTHY 6:3–19

3 If anyone teaches false doctrines and does not agree to the sound instruction of our Lord Jesus Christ and to godly teaching, 4 he is conceited and understands nothing. He has an unhealthy interest in controversies and quarrels about words that result in envy, strife, malicious talk, evil suspicions 5 and constant friction between men of corrupt mind, who have been robbed of the truth and who think that godliness is a means to financial gain. 6 But godliness with contentment is great gain. 7 For we brought nothing into the world, and we can take nothing out of it. 8 But if we have food and clothing, we will be content with that. 9 People who want to get rich fall into temptation and a trap and into many foolish and harmful desires that plunge men into ruin and destruction. 10 For the love of money is a root of all kinds of evil. Some people, eager for money, have wandered from the faith and pierced themselves with many griefs.

11 But you, man of God, flee from all this, and pursue righteousness, godliness, faith, love, endurance and gentleness.

12 Fight the good fight of the faith. Take hold of the eternal life to which you were called when you made your good confession in the presence of many witnesses. **13** In the sight of God, who gives life to everything, and of Christ Jesus, who while testifying before Pontius Pilate made the good confession, I charge you **14** to keep this command without spot or blame until the appearing of our Lord Jesus Christ, **15** which God will bring about in his own time—God, the blessed and only Ruler, the King of kings and Lord of lords, **16** who alone is immortal and who lives in unapproachable light, whom no one has seen or can see. To him be honor and might forever. Amen. **17** Command those who are rich in this present world not to be arrogant nor to put their hope in wealth, which is so uncertain, but to put their hope in God, who richly provides us with everything for our enjoyment. **18** Command them to do good, to be rich in good deeds, and to be generous and willing to share. **19** In this way they will lay up treasure for themselves as a firm foundation for the coming age, so that they may take hold of the life that is truly life.

Shaping Our Wealth Around False Doctrine

Paul wrote 1 Timothy to address the problem in the early church of false teachers and their false doctrines. In chapter 1, Paul wrote of those who "teach false doctrines" (1 Timothy 1:3), "devote themselves to myths and endless genealogies" (1 Tim. 1:4), and have "shipwrecked their faith" (1:19). In chapter 4, Paul wrote of those who "will abandon the faith and follow deceiving spirits" (4:1). Paul called them "hypocritical liars" (4:2). In chapter 6, Paul addressed a specific false doctrine—those who "think that godliness is a means to financial gain" (6:5).

The false doctrine "that godliness is a means to financial gain" has been promoted by some leaders in the church since the first century. It has especially been prevalent in the twentieth and twenty-first centuries in affluent societies like America. This false doctrine has been labeled *the prosperity gospel*. Those teaching the *prosperity gospel* promote the false doctrine that the highest good for people is more money, better health, and success in every endeavor of life. Some of these teachers will presumptuously pronounce over their congregants seven years of blessing, as if their pronouncement will guarantee these blessings.

Paul described the teachers "who think that godliness is a means to financial gain" as people who are "conceited and understand[s] nothing" (6:4). Paul said that they had "been robbed of the truth" (6:5). He also said that they wanted "to get rich" (6:9) and loved money (6:10). The teachers of *the prosperity gospel* in the twenty-first century are the ones who love money and are getting rich. They are the ones with the multi-million dollar mansions, expensive cars, airplanes, and extravagant lifestyles.

A cartoon in a magazine showed two wealthy businessmen eating an exotic lunch in an expensive restaurant. One man had a look of horror on his face. He said, "I had the most terrifying dream last night. I dreamed the value of the dollar had slipped so low that it was no longer worth worshipping."

The false doctrine Paul was addressing is the doctrine of shaping our lives around the worship of wealth. When we shape our wealth around false doctrine we become "conceited" and "understand[s] nothing." Jesus taught that those who think "godliness is a means to financial gain" are promoting a false doctrine that does not work. In Matthew 6:24, Jesus said, "No man can serve two masters. Either he will hate the one and love the other, or he will be devoted to one and despise the other. You cannot serve both God and Money."

Shaping Our Wealth Around Sound Doctrine

Our Christian faith must be shaped around sound doctrine. Paul wrote in 2 Corinthians 2:17, "Unlike so many, we do not peddle the word of God for profit. On the contrary, in Christ we speak before God with sincerity, like men sent from God." Speaking before God with sincerity means speaking the same sound doctrine without distinction to a person's wealth.

Sometimes Christian leaders fall into the trap of favoring those who give large sums of money to support Christian causes. This goes directly against biblical teachings. Paul taught in 2 Corinthians 8:12, "For if the willingness is there, the gift is acceptable according to what one has,

A THEOLOGY OF WEALTH

A theology of wealth must begin with creation. Paul said, "For we brought nothing into the world, and we can take nothing out" (1 Tim. 6:7). When we came into the world, everything else was already here. It was here because God created it. Psalm 24:1 reminds us, "The earth is the LORD'S, and everything in it, the world, and all who live in it."

Wealth consists of things and is generated by things. And all things were created by God. Therefore, everything that exists belongs to God. We are simply managers or stewards of God's things while we are in this world. Our responsibility for these things is determined by God, not by any of our world's standards. These things will still be here when we are gone (Luke 12:13–21).

In the end, we will not be judged by the things we have or don't have but by how we used the things we had. In the parable of the final judgment in Matthew 25:31–46, the only difference between the blessed and the cursed was how they used the things, the wealth, God had given them.

not according to what one does not have." The most powerful example of financial giving in the New Testament is that of the widow's offering cited in Luke 21:1–4. Jesus said, "she out of her poverty put in all she had to live on" (Luke 21:4).

Sound doctrine begins with an emphasis on godliness. Paul told Timothy to remind those who were wealthy "not to be arrogant nor to put their hope in wealth, which is so uncertain, but to put their hope in God, who richly provides us with everything for our enjoyment" (1 Tim. 6:17).

The sound doctrine of godliness, putting our hope in God for everything, promotes the proper use of material wealth. The false teachers were using God to get wealth rather than using wealth to witness to God. Paul taught that shaping our wealth around sound doctrine meant "to do good, to be rich in good deeds, and to be generous and willing to share" (6:18). There is nothing wrong with having wealth, but sound doctrine teaches that we are to use wealth to serve God rather than having our wealth use us, causing us to "fall into temptation and a trap, and into many foolish and harmful desires that plunge men into ruin and destruction" (6:9). People should use their wealth with a humble spirit, remembering that "we brought nothing into the world, and we can take nothing out of it" (6:7).

Paul taught that "godliness with contentment is great gain" (6:6). The word translated "contentment" is a compound word meaning *to rule the self* or *to be self-sufficient*. It is used in the New Testament to denote one's independence of circumstances. Paul used this word in Philippians 4:11, "I am not saying this because I am in need, for I have learned to be *content* whatever the circumstances" (italics added for emphasis).

Contentment comes from living God's way, from shaping one's wealth around sound doctrine rather than the false doctrine of affluence. The "great gain" of the godly use of wealth is the sufficiency found in Jesus Christ.

Further, the "great gain" found in the godly use of wealth manifests itself in laying "up treasures for themselves as a firm foundation for the coming age" and thus taking "hold of the life that is truly life" (1 Tim. 6:19). These spiritual blessings and realities come only with the proper use of wealth. Solomon wrote, "Whoever trusts in his riches will fall, but the righteous will thrive like a green leaf" (Proverbs 11:28).

How We Shape Our Wealth Around Sound Doctrine

Shaping our wealth around sound doctrine calls for guidance by a biblical plan. Every believer should have a biblical getting plan, a biblical spending plan, and a biblical giving plan.

There is nothing wrong with making or having money. One has to make money in order to use money.

But in getting wealth one needs to have the right motive, to be living according to sound doctrine. Paul warned about getting wealth for the wrong purposes: "People who want to get rich fall into temptation and a trap and into many foolish and harmful desires that plunge men into ruin and destruction. For the love of money is a root of all kinds of evil. Some people, eager for money, have wandered away from the faith and pierced themselves with many griefs" (1 Tim. 6:9–10). It has been said that where one person has been ruined by adversity, thousands have been destroyed by prosperity.

> ## THINGS TO DO ABOUT WEALTH
>
> - Examine your plan for relating to your wealth
> - Practice putting your hope in God daily
> - Remember the ways God provides wealth for your enjoyment
> - Explore opportunities to be generous with your wealth
> - Express thanks to God daily for God's provision

Jesus understood that people need the things God has placed in this world. Matthew 6:31–33 states, "So do not worry, saying, 'What shall we eat?' or 'What shall we drink?' or "What shall we wear?' For the pagans run after these things, and your heavenly Father *knows that you need them*. But seek first his kingdom and his righteousness, and all these things will be given you as well" (italics added for emphasis).

A good getting plan for a believer will involve answering sober questions like these: *How will I earn my money? How will I protect my health, my family, my friends, and my relationship with God in the way I earn my money?*

How we shape our wealth around sound doctrine will also involve a good spending plan. What kinds of things will money buy for me to make me healthier and happier?

Further, a good giving plan will address this question: *How much of what I make will I give to help others?* Jesus said in Luke 6:38, "Give, and it will be given to you. A good measure, pressed down, shaken together and running over, will be poured into your lap. For with the measure you use, it will be measured to you."

Paul told Timothy to "command those who are rich . . . to be generous and willing to share" (1 Tim. 6:17–18). One of the greatest and most destructive problems facing our world today is the inequality of wealth. According to one estimate, the combined wealth of the world's richest 1000 people is almost twice as much as the poorest 2.5 billion. The richest 20 percent of the population of the world consumes 90 percent of the goods produced while the poorest 20 percent consume 1 percent. Almost everywhere in the world (including the United States), inequality in wealth is growing fast and that means that the rich, and particularly the very rich, are getting richer, whereas the poor, and particularly the very poor, are getting poorer.[1] James warned in James 5:1–6 that people who "have lived on earth in luxury and self-indulgence" while not treating their workers fairly had fattened themselves "in the day of slaughter."

It is imperative that Christians lead the way in having a good, solid, biblical giving plan. The psalmist reminds us in Psalm 112:5, "Good will come to him who is generous and lends freely, who conducts his affairs with justice."

Implications and Actions

The Bible is filled with instructions on the source of money and the use of money. Money and wealth impact every area of one's life, whether one is a Christian or a non-Christian. According to Paul's writings in 1 Timothy 6, contentment is possible only through godly living. And godly living is inextricably tied to the use of one's material wealth.

It is totally unbiblical to teach that becoming a believer in Jesus Christ is the same as winning the lottery. Using the Christian faith as a means to get rich is a sure road to spiritual ruin and destruction. But using our wealth for good deeds and generosity is a sure road to contentment, and "the life that is truly life" (1 Tim. 6:19).

QUESTIONS

1. Why do you think some people are attracted to *the prosperity gospel*?

2. What is your greatest barrier to being generous?

3. Can you recall an incident in your church life in which a wealthy person was exalted above all others? How did that make you feel?

4. Why is "the love of money . . . a root of all kinds of evil" (6:10)?

NOTES

1. Zygmunt Bauman, *Does The Richness of the Few Benefit Us All?* (Malden, MA: Polity Press, 2013). See also Joseph E. Stiglitz, *The Price of Inequality* (New York: W.W. Norton and Company, 2013), http://www.forbes.com/sites/laurashin/2014/01/23/the-85-richest-people-in-the-world-have-as-much-wealth-as-the-3-5-billion-poorest/, and/or http://www.usatoday.com/story/news/world/2014/01/20/davos-2014-oxfam-85-richest-people-half-world/4655337/ (websites accessed 1/30/2014).

FOCAL TEXT
2 Timothy 1:6–14; 2:1–15

BACKGROUND
2 Timothy 1—2

MAIN IDEA
Paul called Timothy to focus again on serving Christ and to keep on being faithful.

QUESTION TO EXPLORE
What encouragement do you need today to wake up and get going again in serving Christ?

STUDY AIM
To decide to awaken again to serving Christ and to keep on being faithful

QUICK READ
Christians are encouraged to wake up and serve Christ faithfully with a disciplined purpose regardless of what is going on around them.

LESSON TWELVE
Wake Up and Keep Going

Something gets each person to wake up each day. What does it take—an alarm clock, coffee, children, a mind racing with the day's agenda, stress, worry? Productive people heed the wake-up calls and begin worthwhile days. Unproductive people ignore the wake-up calls by hitting the snooze bar of the alarm clock or pulling the pillow over their heads. What wakes you up to service as a Christian?[1]

2 TIMOTHY 1:6–14

6 For this reason I remind you to fan into flame the gift of God, which is in you through the laying on of my hands. 7 For God did not give us a spirit of timidity, but a spirit of power, of love and of self-discipline. 8 So do not be ashamed to testify about our Lord, or ashamed of me his prisoner. But join with me in suffering for the gospel, by the power of God, 9 who has saved us and called us to a holy life—not because of anything we have done but because of his own purpose and grace. This grace was given us in Christ Jesus before the beginning of time, 10 but it has now been revealed through the appearing of our Savior, Christ Jesus, who has destroyed death and has brought life and immortality to light through the gospel. 11 And of this gospel I was appointed a herald and an apostle and a teacher. 12 That is why I am suffering as I am. Yet I am not ashamed, because I know whom I have believed, and am convinced that he is able to guard what I have entrusted to him for that day. 13 What you heard from me, keep as the pattern of sound teaching, with faith and love in Christ Jesus. 14 Guard the good deposit that was entrusted to you—guard it with the help of the Holy Spirit who lives in us.

2 TIMOTHY 2:1–15

1 You then, my son, be strong in the grace that is in Christ Jesus. 2 And the things you have heard me say in the presence of many witnesses entrust to reliable men who will also be qualified to teach others. 3 Endure hardship with us like a good soldier of Christ Jesus. 4 No one serving as a soldier gets involved in civilian

affairs—he wants to please his commanding officer. [5] Similarly, if anyone competes as an athlete, he does not receive the victor's crown unless he competes according to the rules. [6] The hardworking farmer should be the first to receive a share of the crops. [7] Reflect on what I am saying, for the Lord will give you insight into all this. [8] Remember Jesus Christ, raised from the dead, descended from David. This is my gospel, [9] for which I am suffering even to the point of being chained like a criminal. But God's word is not chained. [10] Therefore I endure everything for the sake of the elect, that they too may obtain the salvation that is in Christ Jesus, with eternal glory. [11] Here is a trustworthy saying: If we died with him, we will also live with him; [12] if we endure, we will also reign with him. If we disown him, he will also disown us; [13] if we are faithless, he will remain faithful, for he cannot disown himself.

[14] Keep reminding them of these things. Warn them before God against quarreling about words; it is of no value, and only ruins those who listen. [15] Do your best to present yourself to God as one approved, a workman who does not need to be ashamed and who correctly handles the word of truth.

Wake Up Your Faith in Christ (1:6–7)

Paul was writing to Timothy to re-awaken his faith in and service to Jesus Christ. Timothy was Paul's protégé and also a pastor. Yet Paul had to remind him to "fan into flame the gift of God" (2 Timothy 1:6). The image was of rekindling low burning coals and embers into a roaring fire again.

Many Christians, even leaders, may need this same reminder. These Christians once had a roaring faith that penetrated the darkness and chased away the cold of loneliness but which is now only a dim glow. By picturing the image of fanning the embers back into flame, Paul was illustrating the need for Christians to wake up their passion for Christ instead of remaining in a constant state of Christian malaise. They should not hit the snooze button on their spiritual lives.

Paul laid out three areas in which Timothy and all Christians should be awake and alert. The first is in the area of boldness. Paul's emboldening of Timothy came in the midst of his own arrest and impending execution. He knew that might be an act that would cause even true disciples to become timid. In defiance of that timidity, Paul dared all readers to take up the "spirit of power" 2 Tim. 1:7). God has authority over all things and as God's children, we are co-heirs of God's glory and victory (see Romans 8:16–17). Christians must not be timid about their faith even in the face of difficulty.

Secondly, Paul wrote that Timothy must have a spirit of love. Power without love is tyrannical. Love overcomes fear even better than power does. God-given power emboldens the Christian to endure challenges, but having "a spirit of . . . love" (2 Tim. 1:7) allows a Christian to endure the challenge while lifting up others at the same time.

The third emphasis for awakening the Christian spirit is "self-discipline" (1:7). In the context, Paul was saying that Christians should have the personal discipline to face whatever may come and be ready to live out a life of faithfulness at all times. Together, these three characteristics will bring great confidence to all believers.

"GUARD"

Twice Paul told Timothy to "guard" what had been entrusted to him (1 Timothy 6:20; 2 Tim. 1:14). In between, Paul also wrote that Jesus was guarding something for him (2 Tim. 1:12). Jesus was guarding Paul's salvation. Now with "that day" approaching, Paul was convinced that his deposit into the life and work of Jesus was worth it all. Using the same word, Paul stated that he had passed on to Timothy the deposit that he was holding for Jesus. Paul wanted Timothy to keep the faith as assuredly as Jesus kept Paul's salvation. Later, Paul added that he wanted Timothy to teach others who would become teachers themselves, thereby setting up a chain of deposit keepers (2:2). Each Christian today is a guard of that deposit and ought to pass down the message of Jesus Christ as it was received. There really is no genuine deposit if each generation or Christian changes the message over the years. We must faithfully guard what has been passed down to us.

Keep Going Despite Difficulties (1:8–12)

Paul laid out three reasons for having confidence in the face of difficulty so that followers of Jesus would never be ashamed of their faith. First, no Christian is isolated or alone. Paul said to Timothy, "join with me" (1:8). Paul was already suffering, and he knew that spiritual failure is much more possible when believers are alone. Being a Christian means to be part of a community. By joining together, believers can strengthen one another and help one another endure any kind of difficulty.

A second reason for confidence is that confidence comes from knowing God and what God has already done (1:8–9). Paul listed five foundational strengths in being connected to God: (a) God's power will sustain any believer even through the most difficult suffering; (b) God's salvation provides eternal security even in temporal tragedy; (c) God's calling is the bedrock of every Christian's faith; (d) God's purpose illuminates a plan that is greater than any challenges; and (e) God's grace is sufficient for all things (see 2 Cor. 12:9). These five foundation stones build the pillars of the faith of all believers.

A third reason for confidence is that the gospel is worth whatever proclaiming it costs (2 Tim. 1:10–14). Paul, who was in prison, was not ashamed of the message of salvation through Jesus, and neither should Christians be ashamed of it today (see Romans 1:16).

In verse 13, the words translated "sound teaching" suggest a deliberate, determined, serene confidence that avoids hasty or poor discernment or decisions. In a world of indecision and wishy-washy leadership and faith, "sound teaching" is the truth on which believers can set their lives whatever the cost. Paul encouraged Timothy to keep the prize close to him. He called it the "good deposit" that was entrusted to Timothy. Likewise, all Christians should tightly hold on to this "good deposit" because it is what makes the difference for success or failure as a disciple of Christ. Paul suggested that when things become especially difficult, Christians must rely on the Holy Spirit, who lives within them.

Keep Living and Serving with Disciplined Purpose (2:1–15)

The second chapter of 2 Timothy is filled with imperatives that encourage Christians to live and serve with disciplined purpose: "be strong"

(2:1); "entrust" (2:2); "endure hardship with us" (2:3); "reflect on" (2:7); "remember Jesus Christ" (2:8); "keep reminding them" (2:14); "warn them (2:14); "do your best" (2:15). Paul was giving Timothy, as well as all Christians, his final orders.

Perhaps these emphatic imperatives can be classified into five categories. (1) Be strong (2:1). (2) Be generational (2:2). (3) Be brave (2:3). (4) Be focused (2:4–7). (5) Be biblical, faithful to the gospel (2:8–15). Consider these categories.

First, be strong. It takes strong people to live and serve with purpose. "You then" (2:1) links the previous section about suffering through difficulties with the plan to handle it. The first challenge is to strengthen the mind, spirit, and soul in order to handle whatever may come. Weak people are not able to help others. Only a strong person can significantly help another person. A strong swimmer can save a drowning person. A person with strong finances can help a family member who is struggling with money. A person strong in his or her marriage can help another who is ready to give up on his or her own marriage.

Paul was in prison when he wrote 2 Timothy. Yet, from his spiritual strength, he was helping Timothy to remain strong. Every Christian needs to follow Paul's example and be strong in the Lord.

Second, all Christians would look at the ups and downs of life differently if they would heed the command in verse 2 to be generational—that is, to seek to generate faith and faithfulness in others by passing along the gospel to them. Paul had already mentioned Timothy's mother and grandmother (1:5). He told the young preacher to use what he had been taught to teach others, who would be able to teach a fourth generation. It is not only important that Christians be strong for themselves but that each Christian should see himself or herself as part of something bigger. People who are generational Christians live beyond their current circumstances and serve those coming after them. It is not enough simply to serve others; Christians must lead those whom they serve to become servants themselves. They must lead learners to teach and disciples to become mentors. Each generation will have purpose and meaning as it develops the subsequent generation.

Third, Paul used the image of a soldier to emphasize the need for Christians to be brave in the face of adversity (2:3). Soldiers move into position to attack or defend with discipline and purpose. Bravery

PASSING THE DEPOSIT ALONG

To whom are you passing on the "good deposit" of "sound teaching" (2 Tim. 2:13–14)? How are you passing it along in the following areas of your life:

- To your children or grandchildren? To other children in your life?
- In your church?
- In your community?
- At work or school?

keeps the soldier in place and continuing to do the assigned mission. Likewise, bravery keeps Christians living for Christ and serving Christ's cause. The brave preacher continues to preach when the message is not popular. The brave Christian continues to serve even when life is not easy.

Fourth, then Paul used three examples of how to be focused (2:4): a soldier, an athlete, and a farmer. None of the three are successful if they become distracted or haphazard in their work.

A soldier who gets involved with civilian affairs has lost purpose. Christians lose their purpose when they fail to develop as disciples *of* Christ or when they fail to develop additional disciples *for* Christ. Each Christian has a specific calling on which to focus; anything else is a distraction. That focus includes competing according to the rules, like a worthy athlete. A lack of focus leads competitors to take shortcuts or to look for illegal advantages. Instead, the contestant should focus on a disciplined regimen to become the best athlete possible.

Christians who neglect a daily spiritual regimen are like athletes who are not properly disciplined for the contest. Instead, however, of losing a ribbon or laurel-leafed crown, the lost prize may be the faith or souls of others.

The third illustration is that of a farmer who gets to share in the productivity of the land as a result of hard work. A farmer who is not hard-working will not enjoy any real success. Christians who do not have a faith lived with discipline and purpose will never enjoy the spiritual success that God wants for people. They wonder why they never have real spiritual power, why they have not been part of a revival, or why things always seem to go poorly. Perhaps they were spiritually distracted, took spiritual shortcuts, or neglected the focused diligence of faith.

Finally, be biblical, for "God's word is not chained" (2:9). The core component of real faith is that Jesus died and rose again. Whatever happens to God's people, God's word will not fail. Christians can take confidence in the truth of the Scripture as the mind and direction of God for God's people. Therefore, Christians must keep Scripture as the bedrock foundation of all faith. Finally, Christians must show themselves to be "approved" (2:15) in handling God's word. More than finding some new way of doing Christianity, a Christian leader who handles the Scripture correctly will simply keep focusing on what the Bible says and means.

Implications and Actions

Many things can keep Christians from being faithful servants of Christ: spiritual passivity, difficulties of life, fear, a lack of focus, a lack of knowledge of the Bible, and more. Paul challenged Timothy to wake up from spiritual doldrums and get busy serving God. He then laid out the plan to follow in the kingdom of God. Paul tells us, too, to wake up, take the responsibilities that are before us, and serve the Lord with all the gusto and strength that Paul asked of Timothy.

QUESTIONS

1. What is another way to say, "fan into flame the gift of God" (1:6)? How can you do that in your life? How can you encourage others to ignite their faith?

2. How might Christians be ashamed of the gospel today? How can we encourage ourselves and our fellow believers in not being ashamed of the gospel?

3. What are some ways that Christians are deficient in their understanding of "sound teaching"?

4. From 2 Timothy 2:2, what does it mean to be a generational Christian?

5. How can you demonstrate that you are "a workman" approved by God?

NOTES

1. Unless otherwise indicated, all Scripture quotations in lessons 1–13 are from the New International Version (1984 edition).

FOCAL TEXT
2 Timothy 4:1–8, 16–18

BACKGROUND
2 Timothy 4

MAIN IDEA
As Paul called Timothy to continued faithful service, Paul testified of a future filled with hope.

QUESTION TO EXPLORE
What can we do when we are discouraged or otherwise question the value of living in faithfulness to God?

STUDY AIM
To reflect on my experiences of God's care in difficult times and what these experiences mean to me

QUICK READ
Hope, the fuel that powers Christian faith and service, is found in the presence of God and in the eternal home that awaits us. So let us remain faithful throughout our lives.

LESSON THIRTEEN
Toward a Future Filled with Hope

Hope is the theme of this Scripture passage and this Bible lesson. But what kind of hope? There's more than one kind. For example, blind hope (which is really no hope at all) is when someone *hopes* to win the lottery. Rather than being genuine hope, that's merely empty wishing with little or no chance of fulfillment. Perhaps another kind of hope is more realistic in character. We may *hope* to succeed in this or that endeavor—perhaps an athletic event, a course of study, a job, or a marriage—and we invest the time and effort into trying to make it happen. Yet another type of hope is Christian hope, the hope that is the centerpiece of this lesson. Christian hope combines realistic hope with the promises of God. Christian hope means trusting God now and waiting with confidence for the return of Christ and for a new eternal home in heaven.

2 TIMOTHY 4:1–8, 16–18

[1] In the presence of God and of Christ Jesus, who will judge the living and the dead, and in view of his appearing and his kingdom, I give you this charge: [2] Preach the Word; be prepared in season and out of season; correct, rebuke and encourage—with great patience and careful instruction. [3] For the time will come when men will not put up with sound doctrine. Instead, to suit their own desires, they will gather around them a great number of teachers to say what their itching ears want to hear. [4] They will turn their ears away from the truth and turn aside to myths. [5] But you, keep your head in all situations, endure hardship, do the work of an evangelist, discharge all the duties of your ministry. [6] For I am already being poured out like a drink offering, and the time has come for my departure. [7] I have fought the good fight, I have finished the race, I have kept the faith. [8] Now there is in store for me the crown of righteousness, which the Lord, the righteous Judge, will award to me on that day—and not only to me, but also to all who have longed for his appearing.

• • • • • • • • • • • • • •

[16] At my first defense, no one came to my support, but everyone deserted me. May it not be held against them. [17] But the Lord stood at my side and gave me strength, so that through me the

message might be fully proclaimed and all the Gentiles might hear it. And I was delivered from the lion's mouth. [18] The Lord will rescue me from every evil attack and will bring me safely to his heavenly kingdom. To him be glory for ever and ever. Amen.

Hope in the Presence of God (4:1–5)

Paul looked beyond his temporary challenges. He realized that his time on earth was nearing its end. Like Moses, who peeked over into the Promised Land,[1] Paul was glancing beyond the limited realities of this world and was seeing new spiritual realities that offered the real hope that changes everything in Christian service. He presented five realities that will bring hope to all Christians: (1) We are in the presence of God the Father, who is the Creator of and Sustainer of all things and yet is aware of the smallest things in our lives (2 Timothy 4:1). What encouragement to know that we are in the presence of God at all times, even in the most difficult! (2) We are in the presence of Christ Jesus also (2 Tim. 4:1). Jesus is God in human flesh. He is the way that God became most intimately aware of our plight. Thus, it is especially encouraging to know that Jesus is with us always. He is our Redeemer and our Savior. (3) We will all be judged (4:1). Verse 1 says that it does not make a difference whether we are living or dead when the judgment comes; every person will be judged. Judgment may seem like an unwanted reality but not for the Christian who is dedicated in Christian service. (4) Jesus' "appearing" is still to come (4:1). Jesus is coming back. We can have real hope in the return of Jesus. The return of Christ (along with the resurrection) anchors the hope that Christians have. Death is not final, and no matter what happens in this world, it will all come to an end when Jesus returns. (5) The kingdom awaits those who believe in Jesus. This world is not the home of Christians, and the end of life in this world is not the end of existence. Christian hope is eternal hope. It is not wishing that something *might* happen, but it is knowing that it *will* happen.

With the backdrop of these five realities, Paul gave Timothy five commands. The first was to "Preach the Word" (4:2). Christians should know the Word of God, obey the Word of God, and share the Word of God. Paul told Timothy to be prepared at all times to share God's message. He described three uses of Scripture (to "correct, rebuke and encourage," 4:2) to demonstrate a balanced approach of using the Bible practically for everyday life. When someone has gotten out of line, to "correct" them is to use Scripture to lead them back into line. It is less forceful than the second verb "rebuke," which is when the Scriptures are used more as a flashing warning light to get the attention of someone who has wandered far from the truth. The third word has a positive tone, using God's word to "encourage" Christians. All of this is to be done with patience and careful instruction.

The second command Paul gave was "keep your head" (4:5). Life will most certainly throw one tough thing after another in a dizzying fashion. Paul's wise and practical advice to "keep your head" is based on the fact that God is aware of all things and protects his people. Christians can be confident and resilient even on the roughest days.

The third command is to "endure hardship" (4:5). Paul experienced many difficulties, and he knew that Timothy and the young church would face their own adversity in the days to come. Even so, with a vision of God's nearness and the final reward of heaven, all things were bearable. Paul's example of enduring faith was fueled by his future hope. He set that same hope before Timothy as the target for Timothy's faithfulness.

The fourth command from Paul was for Timothy to "do the work of an evangelist" (4:5). Doing "the work of an evangelist"—sharing God's good news—does two things. Directly, it offers hope to the hopeless by showing them the true path of life. Indirectly, as one is involved in the new spiritual birth of another, the faith of the evangelist is strengthened.

Finally, the last command is a catchall for any minister, to "discharge all the duties of your ministry" (4:5). Don't neglect fulfilling any part of God's call to service.

Hope That Finishes Well (4:6–8)

Paul offered hope as he illustrated his upcoming death by using the Old Testament imagery of a drink offering (Numbers 15:5–6, 10; 28:7). A drink offering consisted of wine being poured out as an auxiliary offering with the other offerings. Paul would never replace or dilute the

---

MARK

Paul's dislike or distrust of Mark was so strong that it broke up the missionary team of Paul and Barnabas (Acts 15:36–41). Mark would go on to serve under Barnabas and Peter. The latter even referred to him as his "son" (1 Peter 5:13).

Second Timothy was most likely Paul's last letter. Somewhere along the way, Paul went from a severe distrust of Mark to asking Timothy to "get Mark and bring him with you" because "he is helpful to me in my ministry" (2 Tim. 4:11).

Mark went from being rejected by Paul to being a help in Paul's ministry. What a message of hope in this story of hope! Is there a Mark in your life who needs a chance at redemption?

---

significance of the sacrifice of Christ, but he was saying that his own life was like an auxiliary offering to God. Jesus was the main blood offering, but Paul's acts of service would also be a pleasant aroma to the Lord.

Paul then used a second image to further describe his death. The word translated "departure" has a military connotation. It referred to lifting the anchor of a warship or to breaking up the army's encampment, with the purpose of heading home. Imagine the activity of the day, every soldier doing what needed to be done but with the excitement and anticipation of heading home. Paul was readying himself as well as Timothy and the ancient church for his own departure that would indeed take him home.

Verse 7–8 are popular verses by themselves, but they are even richer when compared to Acts 20:22–24. Paul had been the pastor of the church at Ephesus for three years (Acts 20:31). After he had ministered in other places, he stopped there briefly on his way to Jerusalem. On his visit Paul gave a heart-wrenching farewell speech to the Ephesian church leaders (Acts 20:18–35). Paul was leaving Timothy behind in that group of Ephesian leaders (see Acts 20:4). Finally, in 2 Timothy, Paul was able to confidently remind Timothy that he had indeed "fought the good fight . . . finished the race," and "kept the faith" (2 Tim. 4:7). Paul's testimony extends hope to all followers of Christ that we, too, can finish well. He further offers hope to all believers with the promise of a "crown of righteousness" that will be the reward for all who finish well and long for the return of Jesus.

Hope in the Heavenly Kingdom (4:16–18)

Paul had been deserted by everyone except Luke (2 Tim. 4:10–11, 16) and stood alone at his "first defense" (4:16). Like Jesus when alone and on trial for his life, Paul was ready to forgive those who had deserted him. Imagine Paul standing with confidence alone in the courtroom, poised because he knew the Lord was standing by his side.

Paul's final hope was to be realized no matter what any person could do to him. He had already escaped "the lion's mouth" once (4:17). He knew there would be other "evil attack[s]" (4:18), and one would finally take his life. Yet he wrote that the Lord who had stood by his side would deliver him from every one of those attacks. The final hope was not in that he would escape the attacks altogether, but that true deliverance awaited him even if his life would be taken. He knew that God was going to bring him "safely to his heavenly kingdom" (4:18). In this verse, the words translated "heavenly kingdom" refer to that which lies on the other side of death.[2] Paul saw his death as the opportunity to enter into heaven and into the presence of God himself.

Implications and Actions

All of us have our own set of distractions and discouragements, but let us find the same hope that Paul did. Our hope is found in the presence of God with us at all times, even if all others should desert us. Our hope is found in the promise of our eternal home and the reward that awaits us there.

Our hope should spur us on to finish well. No runner wins a race by running well for three quarters of the race. A race is won only when the runner gives all he or she has within to reach the finish line. Likewise, all Christians must seek to finish this life's journey well. There cannot be any quitting or retiring from the calling Christ has on our lives. He will be beside us to help us finish well even when to do so seems extraordinarily trying. Let us fight the good fight, finish the race, and keep the faith!

Some themes of the Bible seem very practical, and some themes seem more philosophical or theological. Which description applies to the theme of hope? Hope is one of the most practical subjects in the Bible. Biblical hope provides reason for living faithfully when we are tempted to be unfaithful in marriage, dishonest in business, or weak in our commitment when it is challenged. Keep hoping.

QUESTIONS

1. How does recognizing that we live in the presence of God provide hope?

2. How well do you "keep your head" in difficult times (2 Tim. 4:5)? What can we do to increase the possibility of our doing that?

3. Consider the meaning of "departure" in 2 Timothy 4:6. How do you see this passage as being helpful to someone dealing with his or her own approaching death or the death of a loved one?

4. Which of these two encourages you more in your faith: (1) living faithfully now in the kingdom of heaven or (2) looking with faith toward the heavenly kingdom?

NOTES

1. Deuteronomy 34.

2. The words translated "heavenly kingdom" are different from the words translated "the kingdom of heaven" in the Gospel of Matthew.

Our Next New Study
(Available for use beginning December 2014)

THE GOSPEL OF JOHN:
Believe in Jesus and Live!

How to Order More Bible Study Materials

It's easy! Just fill in the following information. For additional Bible study materials available both in print and online, see www.baptistwaypress.org, or get a complete order form of available print materials—including Spanish materials—by calling 1-866-249-1799 or e-mailing baptistway@texasbaptists.org.

Title of item	Price	Quantity	Cost
This Issue:			
Letters to the Ephesians and Timothy—Study Guide (BWP001182)	$3.95	_____	_____
Letters to the Ephesians and Timothy—Large Print Study Guide (BWP001183)	$4.25	_____	_____
Letters to the Ephesians and Timothy—Teaching Guide (BWP001184)	$4.95	_____	_____
Additional Issues Available:			
14 Habits of Highly Effective Disciples—Study Guide (BWP001177)	$3.95	_____	_____
14 Habits of Highly Effective Disciples—Large Print Study Guide (BWP001178)	$4.25	_____	_____
14 Habits of Highly Effective Disciples—Teaching Guide (BWP001179)	$4.95	_____	_____
Growing Together in Christ—Study Guide (BWP001036)	$3.25	_____	_____
Growing Together in Christ—Teaching Guide (BWP001038)	$3.75	_____	_____
Guidance for the Seasons of Life—Study Guide (BWP001157)	$3.95	_____	_____
Guidance for the Seasons of Life—Large Print Study Guide (BWP001158)	$4.25	_____	_____
Guidance for the Seasons of Life—Teaching Guide (BWP001159)	$4.95	_____	_____
Living Generously for Jesus' Sake—Study Guide (BWP001137)	$3.95	_____	_____
Living Generously for Jesus' Sake—Large Print Study Guide (BWP001138)	$4.25	_____	_____
Living Generously for Jesus' Sake—Teaching Guide (BWP001139)	$4.95	_____	_____
Living Faith in Daily Life—Study Guide (BWP001095)	$3.55	_____	_____
Living Faith in Daily Life—Large Print Study Guide (BWP001096)	$3.95	_____	_____
Living Faith in Daily Life—Teaching Guide (BWP001097)	$4.25	_____	_____
Participating in God's Mission—Study Guide (BWP001077)	$3.55	_____	_____
Participating in God's Mission—Large Print Study Guide (BWP001078)	$3.95	_____	_____
Participating in God's Mission—Teaching Guide (BWP001079)	$3.95	_____	_____
Profiles in Character—Study Guide (BWP001112)	$3.55	_____	_____
Profiles in Character—Large Print Study Guide (BWP001113)	$4.25	_____	_____
Profiles in Character—Teaching Guide (BWP001114)	$4.95	_____	_____
Genesis: People Relating to God—Study Guide (BWP001088)	$2.35	_____	_____
Genesis: People Relating to God—Large Print Study Guide (BWP001089)	$2.75	_____	_____
Genesis: People Relating to God—Teaching Guide (BWP001090)	$2.95	_____	_____
Ezra, Haggai, Zechariah, Nehemiah, Malachi—Study Guide (BWP001071)	$3.25	_____	_____
Ezra, Haggai, Zechariah, Nehemiah, Malachi—Large Print Study Guide (BWP001072)	$3.55	_____	_____
Ezra, Haggai, Zechariah, Nehemiah, Malachi—Teaching Guide (BWP001073)	$3.75	_____	_____
Psalms: Songs from the Heart of Faith—Study Guide (BWP001152)	$3.95	_____	_____
Psalms: Songs from the Heart of Faith—Large Print Study Guide (BWP001153)	$4.25	_____	_____
Psalms: Songs from the Heart of Faith—Teaching Guide (BWP001154)	$4.95	_____	_____
Jeremiah and Ezekiel: Prophets of Judgment and Hope—Study Guide (BWP001172)	$3.95	_____	_____
Jeremiah and Ezekiel: Prophets of Judgment and Hope—Large Print Study Guide (BWP001173)	$4.25	_____	_____
Jeremiah and Ezekiel: Prophets of Judgment and Hope—Teaching Guide (BWP001174)	$4.95	_____	_____
Amos. Hosea, Isaiah, Micah: Calling for Justice, Mercy, and Faithfulness—Study Guide (BWP001132)	$3.95	_____	_____
Amos. Hosea, Isaiah, Micah: Calling for Justice, Mercy, and Faithfulness—Large Print Study Guide (BWP001133)	$4.25	_____	_____
Amos. Hosea, Isaiah, Micah: Calling for Justice, Mercy, and Faithfulness—Teaching Guide (BWP001134)	$4.95	_____	_____
The Gospel of Matthew: A Primer for Discipleship—Study Guide (BWP001127)	$3.95	_____	_____
The Gospel of Matthew: A Primer for Discipleship—Large Print Study Guide (BWP001128)	$4.25	_____	_____
The Gospel of Matthew: A Primer for Discipleship—Teaching Guide (BWP001129)	$4.95	_____	_____
The Gospel of Mark: People Responding to Jesus—Study Guide (BWP001147)	$3.95	_____	_____
The Gospel of Mark: People Responding to Jesus—Large Print Study Guide (BWP001148)	$4.25	_____	_____
The Gospel of Mark: People Responding to Jesus—Teaching Guide (BWP001149)	$4.95	_____	_____
The Gospel of Luke: Jesus' Personal Touch—Study Guide (BWP001167)	$3.95	_____	_____
The Gospel of Luke: Jesus' Personal Touch—Large Print Study Guide (BWP001168)	$4.25	_____	_____
The Gospel of Luke: Jesus' Personal Touch—Teaching Guide (BWP001169)	$4.95	_____	_____
The Gospel of John: Light Overcoming Darkness, Part One—Study Guide (BWP001104)	$3.55	_____	_____
The Gospel of John: Light Overcoming Darkness, Part One—Large Print Study Guide (BWP001105)	$3.95	_____	_____
The Gospel of John: Light Overcoming Darkness, Part One—Teaching Guide (BWP001106)	$4.50	_____	_____

The Gospel of John: Light Overcoming Darkness, Part Two—Study Guide (BWP001109)	$3.55	_____ _____
The Gospel of John: Light Overcoming Darkness, Part Two—Large Print Study Guide (BWP001110)	$3.95	_____ _____
The Gospel of John: Light Overcoming Darkness, Part Two—Teaching Guide (BWP001111)	$4.50	_____ _____
The Book of Acts: Time to Act on Acts 1:8—Study Guide (BWP001142)	$3.95	_____ _____
The Book of Acts: Time to Act on Acts 1:8—Large Print Study Guide (BWP001143)	$4.25	_____ _____
The Book of Acts: Time to Act on Acts 1:8—Teaching Guide (BWP001144)	$4.95	_____ _____
The Corinthian Letters—Study Guide (BWP001121)	$3.55	_____ _____
The Corinthian Letters—Large Print Study Guide (BWP001122)	$4.25	_____ _____
The Corinthian Letters—Teaching Guide (BWP001123)	$4.95	_____ _____
Galatians and 1&2 Thessalonians—Study Guide (BWP001080)	$3.55	_____ _____
Galatians and 1&2 Thessalonians—Large Print Study Guide (BWP001081)	$3.95	_____ _____
Galatians and 1&2 Thessalonians—Teaching Guide (BWP001082)	$3.95	_____ _____
Hebrews and the Letters of Peter—Study Guide (BWP001162)	$3.95	_____ _____
Hebrews and the Letters of Peter—Large Print Study Guide (BWP001163)	$4.25	_____ _____
Hebrews and the Letters of Peter—Teaching Guide (BWP001164)	$4.95	_____ _____
Letters of James and John—Study Guide (BWP001101)	$3.55	_____ _____
Letters of James and John—Large Print Study Guide (BWP001102)	$3.95	_____ _____
Letters of James and John—Teaching Guide (BWP001103)	$4.25	_____ _____

Coming for use beginning December 2014

The Gospel of John: Believe in Jesus and Live!—Study Guide (BWP001187)	$3.95	_____ _____
The Gospel of John: Believe in Jesus and Live!—Large Print Study Guide (BWP001188)	$4.25	_____ _____
The Gospel of John: Believe in Jesus and Live!—Teaching Guide (BWP001189)	$4.95	_____ _____

Standard (UPS/Mail) Shipping Charges*			
Order Value	Shipping charge**	Order Value	Shipping charge**
$.01—$9.99	$6.50	$160.00—$199.99	$24.00
$10.00—$19.99	$8.50	$200.00—$249.99	$28.00
$20.00—$39.99	$9.50	$250.00—$299.99	$30.00
$40.00—$59.99	$10.50	$300.00—$349.99	$34.00
$60.00—$79.99	$11.50	$350.00—$399.99	$42.00
$80.00—$99.99	$12.50	$400.00—$499.99	$50.00
$100.00—$129.99	$15.00	$500.00—$599.99	$60.00
$130.00—$159.99	$20.00	$600.00—$799.99	$72.00**

Cost of items (Order value) _____

Shipping charges (see chart*) _____

TOTAL _____

*Please call 1-866-249-1799 if the exact amount is needed prior to ordering.

**For order values $800.00 and above, please call 1-866-249-1799 or check www.baptistwaypress.org

Please allow three weeks for standard delivery. For express shipping service: Call 1-866-249-1799 for information on additional charges.

YOUR NAME _____   PHONE _____

YOUR CHURCH _____   DATE ORDERED _____

SHIPPING ADDRESS _____

CITY _____   STATE _____   ZIP CODE _____

E-MAIL _____

MAIL this form with your check for the total amount to:
BAPTISTWAY PRESS, Baptist General Convention of Texas,
333 North Washington, Dallas, TX 75246-1798
(Make checks to "BaptistWay Press")

OR, **CALL** your order toll-free: 1-866-249-1799
(M-Fri 8:30 a.m.-5:00 p.m. central time).

OR, **E-MAIL** your order to: baptistway@texasbaptists.org.

OR, **ORDER ONLINE** at www.baptistwaypress.org.

We look forward to receiving your order! Thank you!